• HALSGROVE DISCOVER SERIES ➤

EXMOOR

DEBBIE COXON

PHOTOGRAPHS BY MICHAEL HESMAN

HALSGROVE

First published in Great Britain in 2004

Text – copyright © 2004 Debbie Coxon
Photographs – copyright © 2004 Michael Hesman

Title page photograph: *Big skies and amethyst heather – and nothing else in sight.*

British Library Cataloguing-in-Publication Data
A CIP record for this title is available from the British Library

ISBN 1 84114 356 1

HALSGROVE
Halsgrove House
Lower Moor Way
Tiverton, Devon EX16 6SS
Tel: 01884 243242
Fax: 01884 243325
email: sales@halsgrove.com
website: www.halsgrove.com

Printed and bound by D'Auria Industrie Grafiche Spa, Italy

DEDICATION

To Dad

*He prayeth well, who loveth well
both man and bird and beast*
The Rime of the Ancient Mariner

CONTENTS

Map and Acknowledgements   4

Introduction   5

Chapter 1   **A Solitarie Place**   7

Chapter 2   **Bones of the Moor**   15

Chapter 3   **An Ancient Habitat**   23

Chapter 4   **Man's Footprint**   33

Chapter 5   **A Wild Romance**   41

Chapter 6   **Into the Light**   49

Chapter 7   **The Royal Forest**   55

Chapter 8   **Old and New**   63

Chapter 9   **A Living on the Land**   73

Chapter 10   **Of Mines and Men**   83

Chapter 11   **Maritime Exmoor**   89

Chapter 12   **Saints and Sinners**   99

Chapter 13   **Doonery and all That**   107

Chapter 14   **Myth and Mythology**   117

Chapter 15   **Where Now?**   123

Chapter 16   **Exploring Exmoor**   129

Bibliography and Further Reading   144

EXMOOR NATIONAL PARK

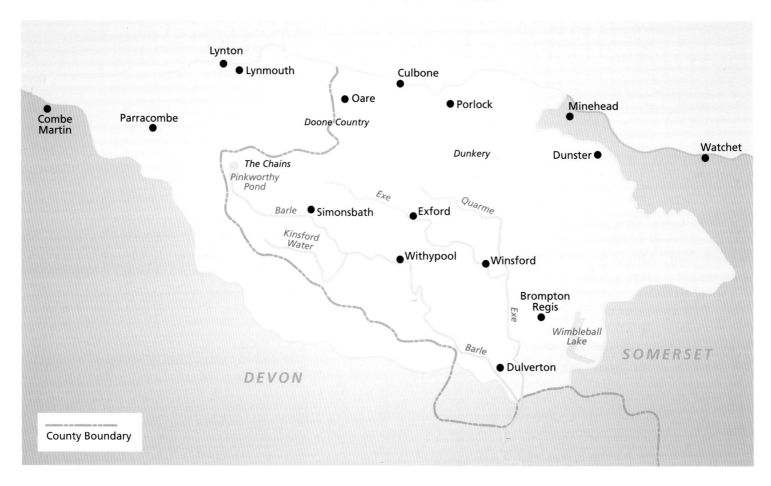

Lynton
● Lynmouth

Culbone ●
Oare ●
Porlock ●
Minehead ●

Combe
Martin ●
Parracombe ●

Doone Country

Watchet ●

Dunkery

Dunster ●

The Chains
Pinkworthy
Pond

Exe
Quarme

Barle ● Simonsbath
● Exford

Kinsford
Water

● Withypool
● Winsford

Brompton
Regis ●

Exe

Wimbleball
Lake

SOMERSET

Barle

● Dulverton

DEVON

━ ━ ━ ━ ━
County Boundary

ACKNOWLEDGEMENTS

To my husband, son and mum, without whom ...
To the many good people of, and good times in, Winsford, without which ...
To fifteen happy years under Exmoor rain, mostly, and sun, sometimes, without which ...
To the many Exmoor experts and lovers who have helped with this book ...

INTRODUCTION

Two artists that I know see Exmoor very differently. One adores its sense of wilderness, the other finds it too 'soft and cuddly'. There is no right or wrong and in some ways they sum up a problem that I rapidly met when researching this book. Everyone knows and loves their own Exmoor.

Some of you who pick up this small volume may have been lifelong residents who know Exmoor intimately. Some may be visitors, new to its charms and anxious to know more. It would be impossible to please everyone. I could not help but be conscious of all the brilliant and more erudite lovers of Exmoor who have gone before. Many volumes packed with knowledge and information have been written and this book cannot better them.

So I have arrived at the hope that in researching this book I have travelled my own journey of discovery – albeit trying to do so in a short space of time in the very worst months of the year! – and can impart

Stonechat.

something new, whoever you are. Friends who know and love Exmoor, who live and farm it, paint it, and walk it far more diligently than I, have all said that you still never truly know it, and to me that sums up the beauty and essence of the place. The smallest of our National Parks, it offers so much, is unique in so many aspects that we shall see, yet manages to retain its mystery, elusiveness and capriciousness.

I would beg to disagree about the soft and cuddly – not least, thinking of the day I did one of Exmoor's more 'cuddly' walks, along the Barle from Simonsbath by way of Cow Castle and Wheal Eliza. The day started fair and half of the walk was lovely, the solitude soothing, though one still felt that life for those who used Cow Castle as a hill-fort, who worked Wheal Eliza, or built the drystone wall that runs for most of the valley, must have been bleak rather than beautiful. Then an Atlantic deluge descended and wilderness ruled. I clambered gratefully into the car, full of admiration for the residents of nearby Horsen Farm, and thanking goodness that home and a hot bath were not too far away, just off the moor.

This is not a walking book or guide as such. There are already plenty of very good ones out there and the many routes, clearly marked on the Ordnance Survey map, will take you a long way. Some would say the best way to know the moor is on horseback and if you are a rider then no doubt you will already have your favourite bridleways. But you really can experience Exmoor on many levels. If you get no further than a picnic and paddle at Landacre Bridge, soaking up the stunning colours, skies and that lovely sense of time having stood still, if only for a little while, you have felt the magic of Exmoor.

In the fifteen years I have lived here, I haven't, to my shame, got to know it as well as perhaps I should; busy lives and all that. But I have absorbed it. I have met many lovely people who have lived here all their lives (who are unfailingly warm and friendly), and remain fascinated by the mercurially changing light, the towering clouds, the glorious palette of colours – first freshest green beech, gorse and heather, violets and primroses – the fantastic sculptures of the hedgerow tree roots and those graceful stands of windblasted trees. Always, too, there is the presence of those primeval people who left their stone monuments, burial barrows, hill-forts and ancient trackways that we still travel, and what differences they would have seen. Familiarity can never breed contempt.

So I was pleased to be given this opportunity to 'discover' better this place on my doorstep. It is almost inevitable that along the line, some facet of the place dear to someone will have been missed out; certainly it will be impossible to cover everything in detail and with the deep knowledge of the moor's inhabitants. But just as there is much yet to discover about Exmoor's archaeology and history – in itself still shadowy – I think it is fitting that the elusive beauty of this moor should hold something of its mystery back – for in doing so it can remain a place out of time and never be reduced to a 'countryside theme park'. I can only hope that if you are already familiar with Exmoor that I may impart something that perhaps you had missed or always wanted to know; for those who are new to Exmoor I hope I can convey something of its unique spirit.

Debbie Coxon, 2004

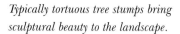
Typically tortuous tree stumps bring sculptural beauty to the landscape.

Chapter 1

A SOLITARIE PLACE

A solitarie place it is, the more commodious for Staggs who keep possession of it

Thomas Gerard, 1633

Thus was Exmoor dismissed by Thomas Gerard and he was not alone. When, early in the eighteenth century, Daniel Defoe's travels brought him in the same direction he was even pithier. 'A filthy barren waste Camden called it and so it is,' he sniffed.

They could be forgiven for seeing little to attract in the remote moorland plateau, as the name makes plain, the moor where the Exe rises. There were no roads to speak of and anyway what was to discover? They were right in some ways; Exmoor is not an easy place; it is very private, its own country, remote and isolated – still, in many ways.

But herein perhaps lies Exmoor's beauty and enduring enigma. Dunkery and Doonery, ponies, purple heather and eye-zapping golden gorse, whorts and wind-blasted beech: these are the quintessential images of calendar and biscuit tin. Some

The Exe winds like a silver thread through the heart of the moor on its long journey to the sea.

potential visitors must think that this is about all there is to it, because Exmoor, strangely – but perhaps thankfully – is the least visited of our National Parks. All the more of it left for those of us for whom Exmoor and its myriad moods means a never-ending journey of discovery.

Look out from Dunkery over a 360 degree panorama on a day when all is impossible technicolour and you might feel that here is the heartbeat, the essence of Exmoor. But perhaps for you it is the exhilaration of looking out from Five Barrows, to Dartmoor, Hartland Point and Bodmin; or perhaps wilderness and solitude at that loneliest and most desolate of spots, where the Exe rises on The Chains; perhaps a feeling of connecting with ancient ancestors at a longstone, with wild ponies from the mists of history grazing nearby. It might be a woodland walk at Tarr Steps; spotting deer at sunset; the glorious,

The gentle swell of Withypool Hill under big skies – quintessential Exmoor.

Though a honeypot, Landacre Bridge (pronounced Lannaker) is simply one of the loveliest spots on Exmoor.

gaudy gorse and heather over Woody Bay; wild waves smashing into Heddon's Mouth; paddling at Landacre Bridge; desolate combes in Doone country; a cream tea or a pint of cider in a thatched pub. There are as many means of discovery: on the hoof, in the saddle of horse or mountain bike; in a kayak, in a vintage car, fishing, painting, taking pictures, writing poetry; the list is endless – each one's Exmoor their very own.

Standing stone at Anstey Common.

You won't as a rule find photographs of Exmoor on a dirge-like November day when the drizzle is lashing sideways across a ghost-grey landscape punctuated only by long-suffering sheep, hedge-banks and tortuously shaped tree stumps depicted in shades of raw sienna and burnt umber. But this is as surely Exmoor, a world where wilderness still rules. Perhaps, with its kaleidoscope of contrasts, its magic lies in being indefinable. Edward Hutton put it:

If a man would know what Exmoor is, let him not waste his breath by climbing Dunkery, seventeen hundred feet and more over the sea. Dunkery stands upon the seaward confines of the moor and will tell him little beyond the lie of the land. Let him march afoot from Porlock to Simonsbath and on to Mole's Chamber, and then back to Exe Head and Pinkerry Pond to Badgery Water; not till he has done this will he have seen the moor ... for there is only the sound of the wind and of running water, only the life of a rare black cock or curlew, a rare pony or herd of deer, only far off, lost in bald downs, a shepherd's hut for dwelling. That is the moor and its face is the face of eternity.

Defining Exmoor is not made easier by the fact that over the centuries its margins seem to have been as blurry as moorland mist. Its creation as a National Park fifty years ago established a definite boundary: an area covering 267 square miles, two-thirds of it in Somerset and a third in Devon, stretching from along the coast of North Devon and West Somerset for about 34 miles between Combe Martin and Minehead, and inland for about 12 miles to Dulverton, the headquarters of the Exmoor National Park Authority. It extends beyond the moorland plateau to include the Brendon Hills, outlying ridges and Minehead and the Vale of Porlock. The Countryside Agency's Exmoor Landscape Character Area extends to the Atlantic coast of North Devon, because of the underlying Devonian rocks. The Quantocks which have similar rocks and character were nearly included but were then designated an Area of Outstanding Natural Beauty because the area between them and Exmoor was not considered to be of National Park quality.

Above: *The sparse trees of the high moor stand stark and graceful in their silvery landscape.*

Right: *Exmoor ponies – ancient survivors and rarer than the giant panda.*

Some still refer to the former Royal Forest of Exmoor, immortalised on maps as Exmoor Forest, and now roughly the parish of Exmoor, as Exmoor 'proper'. Historical records make frequent mention of the men and women of the fringe settlements, such as Molland, North Molton and Brayford, whose lives were for centuries intrinsically involved with that of the moor itself. So while the creation of the National Park may have given Exmoor a more cohesive identity at its heartland, it has in defining the edges created the strange situation where places like Molland and North Molton are not quite in and not quite out. The latter's village boundary lies some 400 yards from the edge of the Park whilst its parish stretches up past the Park boundary to the Bronze Age ridge track that formed the boundary of the former Royal Forest of Exmoor and is now where Devon becomes Somerset. Conversely, as little as fifteen years ago, it was said that a good few inhabitants of North Molton had never been 'upover', certainly had never crossed to the other side of the moor, still less identifying themselves in any way with Exmoor.

It is also arguably (flak jacket on here) the case that Exmoorians (were there such a word) of the Somerset two-thirds regard themselves as more 'of the moor' than their Devonian counterparts. Because of this and the scattered and fragmented nature of the community, it is not easy to pinpoint a typical 'Exmoorian' as such, though its character, dialect and a strong sense of 'how it's done in these parts' are brilliantly captured by longtime Exmoor farmer's wife and writer Norma Huxtable. She recalls the days, not so long ago, when women never left the farm and offers 'foreigners' help with phrases such as ' I got a titch of the nadders' (all is not well) 'ort' and 'nort' (something and nothing) and a 'proper maid' (a fine woman).

So Exmoor is enigma over entity. For where Dartmoor presents a powerful complexion, the Lake District dazzles and the Peak District broods magnificently, Exmoor's charms are more quiet and elusive. Like the indigenous deer that so epitomise this remote and for many Britons, unknown area, it does not push its glories forward; discover for yourself if you will.

Beauty in the backyard

It is hardly surprising that here on this small island on a shrinking planet we should be so desirous of peace and wilderness. Exmoor's early visitors and observers would no doubt have snorted with derision. Government observer William Marshall in 1796 described the 'roads' – more like rough tracks – as being 'in a shameful state' but at least seems to have managed to appreciate the landscape – 'The day is set for rain, yet the appearance of the country is delightful beyond description' – but the more common view, like that of Defoe, saw it as barren, desolate, wet and 'much beclouded with thick fogges and mists'.

Strangely, Napoleon, without ever setting foot on this island, was about to change all that. As he pursued his own grand plans for Europe, gentlemen were forced to abandon their fashionable 'Grand Tour' on the Continent. At last writers and artists, the likes of Wordsworth, Coleridge and Turner (see chapter 13) began to

Dunkery in early morning garb.

eulogise about their own backyard and in doing so brought about a sea change in fashionable notions of 'landscape and scenery'.

In his introduction to *Devon Topographical Prints* John Somers Cocks says:

> *... it was not until the latter part of the eighteenth century that the natural British landscape came to be regarded at all. Without an appreciation of nature and the picturesque, the topographical print could at best only consist of views of important architecture, towns or antiquarian remains, with occasional scenes of military or naval importance ... Once this landscape appreciation had begun it spread very rapidly manifesting itself in prose and poetry as well as art.*

By the end of the nineteenth century it was this change of perception, along with of course the publication of R.D. Blackmore's *Lorna Doone,* that would translate into the 'discovery' of Exmoor as a place of beauty, tranquillity, wilderness, and the double-edged sword of the birth of tourism, for Exmoor at any rate.

Now it is a National Park, Exmoor must welcome visitors but thankfully the Park Authority's efforts to keep the worst intrusions of tourism, along with the essential nature of the place, have saved it from the worst ravages and hopefully will continue to do so. It may

Packhorse bridge, Brendon.

be easier to travel about by car and even coach but it is still in the heart of the rolling moorland, in the secret valleys that whisper of ancient times, in the deep lanes where grass grows down the middle, that the real pulse beats, though it can never be a finite state.

Some utter up a thankful prayer; some bemoan the effect of those who do come, needing tea rooms and trails, car parks and cats' eyes. Some groan to see the surfers and families seeking only a golden sandy beach, racing with loaded wallets down the North Devon link road, past the beautiful, unregarded moor as it hugs to itself its mantle of being the West Country's hidden gem. It is perhaps the quietest of the Parks in more senses than one, being the only one of Britain's National Parks without a military presence. Those visitors who do come, however, tend to get the place under their skin and return time and again – or for good as in the case of this author.

Winds of Change

Exmoor's essential air of timelessness is of course not the restful absolute it might seem when you gaze on an old fingerpost, seemingly a part of the landscape. Though there are some who feel that nothing should be changed and Exmoor should indeed exist in some sort of time warp, it is difficult to know just at which moment they would like time to stand still. In fact, the moor, as we shall see, has changed considerably over the past two hundred years or so since it was 'discovered' by those early

travellers, sometimes subtly, sometimes more overtly. It is as impossible to turn back the advent of roads, horse-drawn bus, railway, the car, and bed and breakfast as to control the vissicitudes of farming and fishing, or indeed the rise and fall of the tides.

In the same breath that aforementioned lovers, and particularly older residents of the moor, cite its unspoilt timelessness, they are likely to utter fears for its future, that it has already changed irrevocably, the biggest threat now in their eyes being, whether they are hunting types or no (as they say in these parts), their very own Sword of Damocles, a ban on hunting with dogs. Some feel that their beloved country is in danger of losing its wild and uncharted nature simply from being over-protected. Even before foot and mouth, many farmers had become disillusioned, to put it mildly, by the ever increasing struggle to make ends meet in the face of indifference, or worse hostility, from those at the heart of power. Meanwhile, as shoots become bigger and bigger business, and the countryside is politicised by the hunting debate, not to mention wind farms, the future is uncertain.

But the winds of change have never stopped blowing over Exmoor and through it all this special place has endured and inspired, as we shall see.

Exmoor in wilderness mood, with the Barle frozen in its tracks.

Coastal panorama from the lower slopes of Holdstone Hill.

Chapter 2

BONES OF THE MOOR

Here I trace the bones of the Moor

Mollie Hawcutt

Leave the lush green fringes and within ten minutes you can be lost in Exmoor's unique landscape: scenery made for the skullduggery of the dastardly Doones; of nibbled-smooth rolling hillside dotted with cotton-ball sheep; of deep mysterious wooded valleys or combes carved out to conceal a Doone or two; of hog's-back cliffs, burbling streams and rushing, roaring rivers, fertile vales and broad coastal flats.

Secret valleys that whisper of ancient times.

There is simply no other place like it in upland Britain. But what has shaped what we see today and why is it so different from that other great brooding plateau visible to the south, Dartmoor? Even the most ardent admirer of the scenery might confess to not really knowing what they are looking at. We might walk the Valley of Rocks many times and really be little wiser as to why it is there, gaze on fossils and gain a mere glimpse into times when the

creatures swam in tropical seas, or look at a grassy hump and really not know whether it be nothing more or a hillfort, barrow or spoil heap.

Much of what we see now has been shaped by erosion over some 20 million years or so and man's influence over the last few thousand years. But the basic structure, the geology, is where any landscape starts, and Exmoor's story began over 400 million years ago. (For a more detailed explanation of the geology and guide to making sense of features out in the field, R.A. Edwards' book *Exmoor Geology* is an excellent place to start.)

The bones of the landscape are three east–west ridges that fall gently away at most edges except to the north where the moor becomes cliffs that drop with magnificent aplomb into the Bristol Channel 800ft

Great Hangman (top right), Little Hangman (centre left) and Lester Point (foreground) illustrating exposed bedding.

(250m) or so below – Britain's highest coastline. Great Hangman, near Combe Martin, is the highest cliff on mainland Britain (defining a cliff as having a slope of greater than 60 degrees) though Culbone Hill is 1350ft (314m) but is a mile inland from the sea.

The 'backbone' central ridge, encompassing The Chains and Dunkery Hill – Exmoor's highest point at 1704ft (519m) – is the source of Exmoor's major rivers: the West and East Lyn, Haddeo and Umber flowing north over short, steep courses, while the Exe and the Barle have cut deep, meandering valleys in the southern part of the Park and flow more gently, the former eventually reaching the English Channel. A small corner of the western and south-western Park is drained by the Mole, Bray and Yeo. This southern

dip slope (the gentle side of the escarpment) includes the commons of Molland and Anstey.

It is humbling to think as you stride out that when the rocks of Exmoor were forming – 200 million years before dinosaurs roamed – they were in an area south of the equator, on the southern edge of a mountainous continent that was today's North America and Northern Europe joined together. They were laid down in – and are a remarkably complete record of – the Devonian period, so called after rocks first studied in that county, through into the succeeding Carboniferous period. Oldest are the Lower Devonian Lynton bed – grey slates and sandstones from 400 million years ago – seen in all their glory in the towering cliffs around Lynton. West and east of these it is the dramatically named Hangman Sandstone (Grits) of the Middle Devonian period that, with their resistance to erosion and weathering, are now amongst the highest parts of the moor, including Dunkery, with Selworthy Beacon and Croydon Hill to the east.

Around Porlock and Minehead we see much younger rocks of Triassic (251 million years) and Jurassic (205 million years) age; the Vale of Porlock for instance is composed of Permian, Triassic and Jurassic rocks. Triassic rock can be seen in the tower of Oare church.

The reason that Exmoor is so very different from Dartmoor and the neighbouring Cornish moors lies in the nature of the rock, the latter being granite which began as a molten mass that cooled into crystals, known as igneous rock. Exmoor's underlying rock is sedimentary – formed, as the name implies, from sediments in water or from desert sands, which were later laid down again and cemented to solid rock. The different sizes of the fragments in the sediments translates into the resulting rock. Mud became shales, sands formed sandstones, and larger particles became grits, breccias and conglomerates; limey deposits became limestone. With all of these found on Exmoor, it becomes easier to see where the variety and contrasts of the landscape originate.

The coast is the best place to see the exposed Devonian rocks. Most accessible is the Valley of Rocks with its shales, sandstones and limestones, and a few fossils. At Heddon's Mouth we can see the transition between the grey-coloured marine sediments of the Lower Devonian and the red desert sandstones of the Middle Devonian. At Combe Martin there are younger Devonian rocks and the trace-fossil *Chondrites*, probably left by a burrowing worm, can be found in the Ilfracombe Slates there, as well as at Woody Bay.

For most of us fossils are very immediate and fascinating and those of Exmoor, though not as abundant and spectacular as on the southern Jurassic Coast of Devon and Dorset, tell their own story. The limestones of the Ilfracombe Slates, for example, derive from former coral reefs of warm, clear seas. Rocks that were formed on land, where there was still little in the way of life – like the Hangman Sandstone – contain few fossils, a few plant fragments and – rarely – the remains of fish. Where sediments originated in the sea or river mouths, as in the Devonian rocks known as Ilfracombe Slates and Lynton Formation – we see more. Fossils of the *Myalina* sea shell can be seen at Combe Martin's Wild Pear Beach and on a seashore walk you might be lucky enough to pick up a pebble containing the fossilised fragment of a crinoid – colonies of creatures known as 'sea lilies'. The Valley of Rocks may also yield a sighting.

Sometimes Exmoor seems almost to glow with colours that owe their existence not just to heather, gorse, beech and bracken but reflect into the clouds from the rocks beneath and back again. Around Combe Martin, in the valley of the Umber, lies a hard band of limestone stained purple with iron minerals and in places weathered to leave the brown mineral umber, which has been quarried for pigment. Another predominating colour, red, seen in the Exmoor sandstones, illustrates a long battle between land and sea, of colliding continents and great upheavals and the 'big squeeze'. Some 400 million years ago when Britain was still south of the equator, South Wales was part of a large desert continent – the so-called 'Old Red Sandstone' continent – because of the red of the sandstones caused by oxidation of the iron compounds in the hot desert. South Devon was beneath a shallow tropical sea with coral reefs and Exmoor lay between the two, sometimes a sandy plain, sometimes underwater.

A landscape is born

It all changed – earth-shatteringly – about 100 million years later when great upheavals caused the northern continent and another, roughly comprising today's South America and Africa, combined to collide. Exmoor, squashed in between, buckled and folded like a concertina. The layers of rock that had been horizontal were heaved up into an arch-like structure, or anticline in geological terms, with its centre running eastwards from Lynton towards Porlock, north of which the rocks generally tilt northwards; to the south of it and thus over most of Exmoor they run mostly to the south. The tremendous force also caused folds, major cracks known as faults, and cleavage, where finer grained rocks, like slate, split along closely spaced fractures. A chain of mountains, possibly as high as the Himalayas, was hurled up over South West England, only to be worn to stumps over the next 100 million years or so. At the same time, volcanic activity forced minerals through the existing rock, which would cause all manner of anticipation and angst when man sought to exploit them millennia later.

All this turbulence, millions of years of changing climates, sea levels and earth movement, left a fairly simple surface structure but one that is complicated in detail. Erosion and the influence of man changed things further. Yet for all that, it seems remarkable how vividly and how much of the underlying geology directly translates into the shape and features of the landscape we see today. Go to Wild Pear Beach, Hurlstone Point, Culver Cliff at Minehead or almost anywhere between Minehead and Baggy Point to see a cross-section of all the strata and the drama of their history.

A relatively calm era dawned with desert climate, lakes that came and went leaving muddy sediments, and the mountains themselves destined to be worn away again, albeit over some 100 millions of years (we move on in big chunks here!). Huge amounts of material were washed down the valleys as scree. In the arid climate of this Triassic era the rocks were 'rusted' to red colours and would later form New Red Sandstones (because they were reworked from the old ones) seen in the Vale of Porlock, near Luccombe, Wootton Courtenay and around Minehead.

Another sea invasion left marine fossils such as ammonites and bivalves that are preserved around Selworthy and Minehead. Another of those 100 million year leaps saw it all lifted out of the sea again and the Exmoor plateau was born. The puzzle is why our plateau stands higher than the surrounding country when to the

west there are identical Devonian rocks that are not high moorland. Current thinking is that a block or 'horst' defined by faults was raised 490–650ft (150–200m) above the adjacent country about 25 million years ago and at the same time slightly tilted. Exmoor, unusually, escaped being buried under the ice sheets that were to cover most of Britain from around 2 million years ago, and as a result bears the remarkable honour of being one of the oldest landforms on the earth's surface, certainly more ancient than the main mountain ranges and continents.

Ice – and easy on the eye

Though the ice sheets that advanced and receded over Britain stopped short of Exmoor, they brought tremendous climate change, with dramatic effects caused by ever changing sea levels and weathering. In the 'periglacial' climate of places such as Exmoor, ice activity produced weathering and erosion of rocks. Though the ground was frozen for long periods, during periods of thaw a surface layer melted and large quantities of frost-shattered rock fragments slid down slopes in a muddy 'porridge.' The resulting

Looking to the hog's-back cliffs of Countisbury Foreland, made up mainly of Hangman Sandstone.

deposits, called 'head' occur almost everywhere on Exmoor and form a layer up to 200ft (60m) on the floor of the Valley of Rocks. The smooth rounded hillsides and hog's-back cliffs so characteristic of the coast between Combe Martin and Minehead owe much of their shape to weathering and erosion. It is thought likely that the Punchbowl – a distinctive bowl-shaped hollow on the northeast side of Winsford Hill – might have been a kind of glacial corrie. Another similar feature is Raven's Nest near Simonsbath which can be reached from the car park at Prayway Head.

The Valley of Rocks, running parallel along the coast between Lynton and Lee Bay, is paradoxically, a brilliant illustrated lesson in Exmoor geology yet in complete contrast to the valleys or indeed anywhere else on Exmoor. A valley that has mislaid its river, and running parallel to the sea, it seems to boast tors and rocky outcrops more reminiscent of Dartmoor and where Castle Rock

Waterfall at Woody Bay.

meets the sea the usual hog's-back shape gives way to a stupendous vertical drop. Geologists have puzzled over its origins and why it lost its river but now reckon that it was part of the valley of the Lyn when it met the coast further west than at present. As the sea rose, eroding the coast and eventually breaking into the valley side at Lynmouth, the East and West Lyn took a new outlet, leaving the old valley floor abandoned. The craggy outcrops, tors and screes that litter the slopes bear testimony to freeze-thaw action during the Ice Age when water froze and expanded in the vertical cracks, known as joints, in the rock, breaking them into the fragments we call screes. Where rocks stood in a drier part of the valley or were less jointed they were

left outstanding as tors. You can get to the Valley of Rocks by road, or from Lynton along North Walk on the north side of Hollerday Hill. Once in the valley, look north (towards the coast) where you will see a line of prominent rocky crags which include 'Rugged Jack,' and, at the western end of the valley, Castle Rock. You should catch a glimpse of the wild goats that live here and, if lucky, spot fossils in the Lynton Formation rocks or in the limestone at the base of the 'Devil's Cheesewring'

Many special features of our lovely landscape are due to changes in sea level, as in the Ice Age. At the coast can be seen waterfalls, some hurtling down cliffs, the Valley of Rocks, the Lyn delta, the shingle ridge and submarine forest at Porlock, while inland we see steep-sided valleys or combes and knolls such as at Flexbarrow and Cow Castle. The valleys show how rivers have cut down in stages as the sea level rose and fell, widening, cutting down and narrowing, then widening again, resulting in the deep combes. Knolls occurred as rivers meandered over flood plains, perhaps before starting to cut down again, around areas of more resistant rock in the valley sides. Where streams have not been able to cut their valleys down to the sea as fast as the rising sea has worn back the coast, waterfalls plunge over the cliffs – an unusual feature worldwide. Hollow Brook at Martinhoe is arguably the highest waterfall in the West Country and among the highest in Britain, dropping 656ft (200m) to the sea via a series of cascades over a quarter of a mile (400m) and two 165ft (50m) drops. Like Sherrycombe, with a fall of about 100ft (30m), it is best seen from a boat trip along the coast but Hanging Water in Woody Bay can be

A paradoxical lesson in geology or simply a stunning place to be – the Valley of Rocks.

Above: *Looking into The Punchbowl at Winsford, thought by some to be a glacial corrie.*

Right: *Porlock shingle ridge, regularly breached by storms.*

seen from the beach. At other times of dropping sea levels in colder parts of the Ice Age, rivers cut down rapidly to the coast, creating deep gorges such as that of the East Lyn.

At Porlock the shifting sea levels are responsible for a 'submarine forest' on the seaward side of the shingle ridge there. It can be seen, though normally only at low tides, and if you able to do a bit of nimble footwork across the cobbles from Porlock Weir. The beach, beloved by artists with its textured stones and man-made groynes, is one of the finest shingle beaches in Britain and also one of the best examples of a 'baymouth bar'. Created by the process of 'longshore drift', westerly winds continually shifting the stones eastward along the coast, it is by its nature ever changing and problematical. Rising sea levels moved the ridge inland – covering the prehistoric forest that was home to Mesolithic people and wild oxen – and eventually closing off part of the bay to form a lagoon or saltmarsh, depending on conditions, now a Site of Special Scientific Interest. But storms and flooding at high tides have caused regular breaches in the shingle ridge and it is now thought that perhaps the groynes meant to stabilise the ridge have actually made it less stable. Thinking has now swung in favour of letting Nature get on and decide whether the area reverts to lagoon or marsh.

River and flood

Sadly, the East and West Lyn will be forever notorious for the calamitous flood of 1952 when 34 people died after 9 inches of rain fell in twelve hours on The Chains. Six inches of rain during the first two weeks of August 1952 had already saturated Exmoor's thin layer of topsoil, leaving it unable to absorb any more water. On the morning of 15 August hazy sunshine seemed promising but by lunchtime the rain had returned with a vengeance, and finally something had to give. Water cascaded down the valley sides, causing many landslips; debris created dams at river bridges which when they burst sent walls of water down the narrow valleys. By teatime, water 12 inches deep was pouring through Lynmouth's streets and the Lyn rivers, which flowed close to properties in the little town, had risen steadily and turned black as they filled with peat. As each blockage upstream burst, surges of water up to 30ft (9.1metres) high carrying boulders, trees, telegraph poles and all manner of debris, hurtled down into the town, tearing the heart out of it. In all millions of tons of water, water equivalent to a flood of the Thames, had been disgorged as the East and West Lyn lost any chance of coping.

Parts of the West Lyn are now a Site of Special Scientific Interest for the features of the flood that they illustrate, such as the boulders weighing up to 50 tons moved by the flood at Glen Lyn Gorge. Major work was done to re-channel the rivers in the town so that never again could it be so vulnerable. Even normally gentle rivers flowing southwards, like the Barle, became agents of destruction in many Exmoor communities; the Barle took with it all but one section of the massive boulders of the ancient clapper bridge at Tarr Steps, undoing the work of Royal Engineers who had just restored it after previous flood damage. In their own way the flood and the normally beautiful, peaceful rivers of the East and West Lyn, wreaked as powerful an effect on the landscape as many of the events of previous aeons.

The peaceful River Barle.

Chapter 3

AN ANCIENT HABITAT

Out on the high moor, with only sheep and crows for company, Exmoor seems far from unique with little else living sharing this wilderness. But Exmoor truly is unique. It is a melting pot of ancient, virtually undisturbed habitats, a last bastion of species driven to extinction elsewhere.

Almost everyone is aware of its two most potent symbols, the red deer – symbol of the National Park and all things Exmoor – and the ponies – and if anything is Exmoor's USP it is these. You are

Exmoor ponies – always a lovely sight.

A361 as juggernauts roar by. Their chocolate-box looks (made up of intensely practical features), and visibility, belie two paradoxical facts; they are the nearest we have to the true wild horse – their zoological importance as such internationally recognised – and amazingly they are rarer than the giant panda.

They are now 'wild' only in that they roam freely over the moor – all the herds are owned – and steps have been taken by the National Park Authority, owners and bodies

likely at almost any time to spot a pretty family group, quietly grazing. Yet it is always a thrill to see them because these ultimate survivors have lived in harmony with the landscape since long before man and embody all that is special about Exmoor itself.

Perhaps, having seen generations come and go, that is why they seem so oblivious and serene, even grazing up to the edge of the

like the Exmoor Pony Society to head off extinction. It is a delicate balance. The Exmoor pony is unique precisely because the strain has remained uncorrupted, which in turn was able to happen because Exmoor remained isolated from outside influences for so long. Too much interference could undo all that but now that the ponies no longer have a working role, it is clear that their precious legacy must be protected, and careful management tries to ensure this.

Above: *Red deer in perfect harmony with its habitat.*

Right: *New arrival.*

The eight herds, comprising some 150 – 200 ponies – are 'managed' by means of the annual autumn 'drift' when, with their foals, they are driven down to the farms where the foals are weaned, and all the ponies are inspected and branded before being returned to the moor for the winter. The fine glossy coat of summer grows into a thick two-layered winter 'greatcoat' that, like the the jut of their brow and the 'toad' eyelids, shields against snow and sheds rain; the fat stores they have built up all though the summer carry them through the harshest of elements. As well as giving so much pleasure to those out enjoying the moorland landscape, there is still a useful role for some of their number, in equestrian pursuits like riding, showing and driving in harness. And they make great family ponies so long as they are properly tamed and trained. They now also 'earn their keep' by keeping down unwanted scrub.

You should spot the best-known group, the Anchor herd, roaming on Winsford Hill. The National Park Authority herds are on Haddon Hill and on its Exmoor Forest estate at Larkbarrow and Warren. Porlock, Withypool, Molland, and West Anstey Commons are also good spots for seeing Exmoor ponies.

Whilst at first sighting the ponies make a charming and pretty scene, we probably all realise that our response goes deeper. They really do encapsulate all that has made Exmoor unique, in its long resistance to the changing fads of the outside world. Ancient, virtually unchanged, wild and free, rare and under threat – they perfectly symbolise their beautiful home.

Much more elusive, though right up there in the public eye, is the red deer herd. Arguably it is often a public from far beyond Exmoor, more concerned with their nearest wine bar and a 'decent red', and you would have to have been living on Mars to know nothing of the controversy now focused on the red deer.

Of red deer and hunting on Exmoor, more later, but whatever your views the two have gone together and are indeed woven into the landscape, since time immemorial. Long before its designation as a Royal Forest, since the last Ice Age, the deer were here and Exmoor is the only place in England and Wales where they have remained continuously in the wild. It is hard to believe that these magnificent creatures, now the largest wild land animals in England, were regarded as pests and almost hunted to extinction. They managed to survive here thanks to their protection as royal game in the Forest but teetered on the brink when it shrank in the thirteenth century and were nearly exterminated – down to the last 60 or so – in the early nineteenth century for the damage they did to crops. Thanks to the action of some landowners they were saved so that now a few thousand live on and beyond the National Park, some 2500 within its boundaries.

Now they can be found anywhere in the National Park and around the fringes, though for the visitor, usually at more of a distance than the ponies. Local residents know where to go, and grow used to them coming right up to their homes, with mixed feelings!

Above: *Stag in velvet – as the new growth of antlers is called.*

Left: *Stags fighting during rut – if you should be lucky enough to see this, keep your distance!*

26

Round-leaved sundew.

Otherwise to see them more closely, except for lucky sightings, you will have to be a bit more dedicated. A moorland safari is a fun and relatively easy way to do it. Other than that, walking off the beaten track around wooded valleys such as those of the Exe, Barle, Horner Water or around West Anstey Common, you may well strike lucky. Go early morning or late in the day, when they are most active, for the best chance.

Normally the stags and hinds stay in separate herds except during the autumn rut or mating period. This is also when the stags 'bell' or roar, a sound that is something on its own! Only the stags grow antlers which are shed in late April – not later than 1 May – the new ones growing immediately. With age the stags acquire more 'points', until they reach old age and start to 'go back'. The calves are born in June and July and are usually dropped in vegetation or by the edge of woodland – but they may as easily choose a cornfield! If you should come across a calf, do not touch it as its mother, who will be nearby, would then reject it. Another rule of Exmoor Forest is that whoever finds a pair of horns may keep them, and it is not unusual for visitors to find a handsome pair.

It is lovely to think of the ponies and deer as ancient survivors in a wild primeval landscape but they have seen Exmoor's wilderness change its coat in many ways and the balance is ever shifting. The open uncultivated moorland that most of us would probably see as truly wild, covering about a quarter of the Park, owes much to 5000 years of clearing and farming by man and the grazing of his animals, mainly sheep. Arguably true wilderness was broadleaved woodland which has now shrunk to just an eighth of the area. Nearest to that earliest state is to be found only on the shore and some sea cliffs out of grasp to fire or grazing sheep, or where heath or grassland occurs naturally because it is too exposed for trees.

Moor and heath

Moors and heaths – the former occurring on wet, acid soil, the latter on free-draining soil – may not be entirely natural but they can claim antiquity of millions of years, and are in many ways special in their own right. On Exmoor can be found 23 of the 80 plus main types of moor and heath, some internationally rare. Moorland, though common in Britain, is surprisingly rare worldwide, so that we have 15 per cent of the global total. The word 'moor', from the Saxon for marsh, occurs on wet, acid soils. On Exmoor, it expanded after the Ice Age but as woodland took over, shrank back to the hill tops and valley bottoms until Bronze Age man appeared in about 1500BC. Thus began the moor and heathland landscape we see. Grazing of sheep and goats prevented woodlands from regenerating, followed by the climate cooling of the Iron Age about 500BC. With the loss of trees, nutrients were washed away from some soils, while others were waterlogged, so creating ideal conditions for moorland. Bog mosses such as sphagnum love such wet conditions and act like a sponge, holding the water and making them even wetter. They also produce acids that inhibit other plants and so can rapidly take over. Because bacteria and other organisms that cause decay cannot survive the acid, wet conditions and oxygen is quickly used up, dead plants just remain, eventually being compressed to form peat. Living plants have to be specially adapted to cope, so some like the round-leaved sundew *(Drosera rotundifolia)* and the rare butterwort *(Pinguicula lusitanica)* gain nutrients by digesting trapped insects. The latter is interesting in that the *lusitanica* part of the name refers to 'lusitanian', an old name for Portugal. Much of the flora of Exmoor, and typical vegetation – heathland and sessile oakwoods – is similar to this part of Europe and Europe's Atlantic seaboard.

Apart from the moss, the moors are mostly grassland, their lower slopes featuring deer sedge, of which Exmoor has more than anywhere else in southern England. Improvement attempts – drainage, heavy grazing and frequent burning – after the Royal Forest was sold encouraged the growth of purple moor grass *(Molinia caerulea)* which now covers much of the former Forest. In some places this is in combination with meadow thistle which is unusual.

Environmentally the peat earns its keep by locking up vast amounts of carbon dioxide, the main 'greenhouse' gas, and by soaking up rainwater, preventing floods, but releasing water when it is needed. The moorland also, of course, supports human 'wildlife' seeking refreshment of body and soul with wonderful scenery, fresh air and closeness to nature!

It seems hardly ideal for wildlife, and the variety is limited but what there is is important and often unusual. The ponies do seem to find it a natural habitat and the deer graze it though woodland is home. Then there are the many small animals that are dinner for the birds of prey and short-eared owls. Other birds are curlew and snipe, sadly not doing so well these days.

What looks like moor may be heath, found in both upland and lowland areas and also on acid soil, the main difference being that its soils are well drained. As the name suggests heather is a typical plant of heaths, along with other small shrubs which are usually well adapted to drought and fire, as well as coping with high rainfall. Though similar heathland is found along the Atlantic seaboard from southern Norway to northern Portugal, Britain has the most as it has the best conditions for the growth of ling, the commonest heathland plant. As with the moorland, internationally this is quite unusual, as reflected in the wildlife; Exmoor is a stronghold for whinchats, the rare heath fritillary butterfly and the bog-loving ivy-leaved bellflower, to name but three examples.

Heath fritillary.

The highest heaths feature a mixture of ling *(Calluna vulgaris)* and whortleberry *(Vaccinium myrtillus)*. It is the former that offers the glorious blaze of purple when it blossoms in autumn, headier still when in combination with golden gorse, a truly eye-popping sight. On Dunkery tormentil, blue heather speedwell, heath spotted orchid, bog pimpernel and milkwort vie for attention. The whortleberry, known elsewhere as bilberry, was traditionally part of the Exmoor calendar and larder, drawing families and gypsies from around the fringes to pick the small purple fruits till their fingers ached. No Exmoor cookbook would be complete without its whortleberry recipes. Lower down, the combination of Western gorse *(Ulex gallii)* in combination with bell heather *(Erica cineria)* and the bristle bent grass *(Agrostis curtisii)*, seen to spectacular effect in August, predominates, along with wavy hair grass *(Deschampsia flexuosa)*. Birds of these heaths are the meadow pipit, wheatear, stonechat and whinchat, along with the less common ring ouzel, merlin and hobby.

Illustration: Sheila Wilkinson

Left: *Devil's bit scabious.*

Above: *Ivy-leafed bellflower.*

Left: *Bog asphodel brings a welcome splash of sunshine to the bleakest parts of the moor.*

29

Bell heather and gorse on Crawter Hill looking towards the Vale of Porlock.

Over a chequered history of climate change, reclamation by man, grazing animals, and environmental pressures such as pollution, Exmoor's moors and heaths, and the wildlife they support, have hung in fine balance, never more so than today. Grazing pressures and nitrates in the air can lead to whortleberry and heather being replaced by grasses, rushes and bracken, while introduced grasses, mosses and rhododendrons threaten to take over. Schemes pioneered by the National Park Authority to temper reclamation, designations of areas by English Nature as Sites of Special Scientific Interest, and ongoing review of burning practices, are all attempting to protect Exmoor's unique habitat. It is an unenviable task.

Controlled burning – or swaling – is employed to maintain the delicate balance of moorland vegetation – here carried out on Trout Hill by ENP rangers.

Rhododendron can be invasive and a problem but it is hard to decry it here.

❧

Chapter 4

MAN'S FOOTPRINT

A morsel of earth now damps in silence the eclat of noisy warriors,
and the green turf serves as a sufficient shroud for kings!

Collinson 1791, II, 20

It is almost inevitable out on Exmoor for the mind to wander. The sun scuds movie-style across burial barrows breaking the horizon, or perhaps a standing stone, and you find yourself lost in another world, wondering how it must have been for those ancient inhabitants. How did they live? And where? Your relatively simple journey would have taken days, with no waymarked route, no A to B even, a ridgeway route perhaps your best hope and who knows what hazards to be encountered.

So much history packed in and palpable that our A to B, or walk with the dog, can be a journey through time. All over this twenty-first century landscape we have prehistoric burial mounds, enigmatic stone settings and circles, prehistoric enclosures, forts, ancient farmsteads and medieval settlements. There are nearly 4000 known archaeological sites and new discoveries are being made all the time. We are lucky that the archaeology of the area has generally escaped destruction by agricultural improvements in past times. There are many areas still to be explored and Exmoor's archaeology is still virtually a raw resource, a Time-team paradise.

Within Exmoor's 400 million year existence, man's sojourn – a mere six or seven thousand years – is positively paltry yet has left a unique and indelible imprint. Down the centuries, it is man's efforts to eke

a living and mark his passing that have honed and shaped from that newly emerged plateau the moor we see today. Paradoxically, so much tangible evidence still holds as many mysteries as answers, which arguably adds to the magic.

The earliest clue to man moving in, the find of stone handaxe near Porlock, points to some presence in the Lower Palaeolithic period perhaps as early as 300,000 years ago. But taken alone it tells us little else and is surrounded by a rather large blank. Not until an Ice Age later and Mesolithic times some 8000 years ago did a much clearer picture start to emerge. Finds of small flint implements called microliths – used for the tips of arrows and spears – around sixty years ago – are more helpful. Britain was by now an island, and in the better climate tundra gave way to woodland, and there was more available food.

One of the richest areas for such finds is in and around Porlock Bay, particularly Hawkcombe Head, Exmoor's oldest archaeological site, dating back around 6000 years, where flints were first found in 1947. Flint does not occur naturally on Exmoor and many of the flints show signs of working, or having been fashioned into particular tools. So the story of people on Exmoor really starts here, a picture of extended family groups, with a hunter-gathering lifestyle,

Late winter afternoon on Fyldon ridge strikes primeval pose.

D. Coxon

roaming across Exmoor. Around them in the dense oak woodlands lived elk, red and roe deer, wild pig and wild cattle or aurochs. Bones of the latter and flints have both been found beneath the submerged forest off Porlock Beach. The hunter-gatherers would also have been able to feast on wildfowl from the salt marsh, crabs and limpets and fish from the sea. These people were probably the first to manage the landscape by burning the woodland margins, encouraging their prey to graze there so that they could more easily hunt them.

In 2003 a two-week excavation at Hawkcombe Head by schoolchildren and students, run jointly by the Exmoor National Park Authority and the University of Bristol, made more exciting discoveries. Over 1000 pieces of flint were recovered and towards the end of the excavation came evidence of occupation; perhaps a hearth site and temporary structure. Such remains are extremely rare in England and more work is in the pipeline.

These people probably wandered the hills for six or seven thousand years before a different age slowly dawned, a more settled way of life, in other words, the first farmers. Again a few artefacts such as flint axes give clues but nothing to firmly indicate any settlement on Exmoor of these Neolithic or Stone Age people. Finds of leaf-shaped and triangular arrowheads around Selworthy Beacon and worked flints at Kentisbury Down, indicate the area being used as a hunting ground by people who probably stayed for a few seasons at least.

Stones and Bones

In complete contrast, somewhere along a somewhat blurry line as the 'ages' that we denote merged slowly, came about a time – the Bronze Age – whose people left for us a relative wealth of visible and highly evocative evidence. These people brought new ideas – from the style of their pottery to the way that they buried their dead – and most importantly a knowledge of working metal for both utilitarian and ornamental use. A necklace from a North Molton barrow – stumbled across by a farmer ploughing – is of Baltic amber

indicating that trade with far-flung places was well established. At once these people seem very real: as architects of the earliest man-made structures on Exmoor – the standing stones, circles and stone settings. Yet more fascinating, they left the great burial barrows – nearly 400 of them – whose immutable and distinctive profiles, so serene on the skyline, draw the ancient world right down into our everyday lives some 3000 to 3500 years later.

The stone monuments, of local sandstone and slate, thought to be Late Neolithic and Early Bronze Age, occur as stone circles, stone rows, stone settings and solitary (or paired) standing stones but, with one or two exceptions, are somewhat elusive. Found mostly in the western half of the National Park where they have escaped man's agricultural 'vandalism', they are usually small stones owing to the nature of the raw material. Though less spectacular than those on Dartmoor, they are fairly comparable in style except for the stone settings, which puzzlingly are unique to Exmoor and have been described as 'without parallel in Britain and Ireland'. Frustratingly, many have been lost and archaeological work is still ongoing.

The exception is without doubt the impressive and for many, most spiritual, of Exmoor's stone monuments, the solitary jag of slate known as the Long Stone at Challacombe. At 9ft (3m) high, it can hardly be better described than by longtime Exmoor dweller Hope Bourne as 'a dark finger thrusting up from the sullen earth'. We just don't know what it signifies but it stands in the vicinity of other stone settings and some of the most dramatic barrows on Exmoor so it seems likely that it had some religious or ritual purpose. Fittingly, for to reach it will involve a reasonably challenging walk, crossing high, rough and usually soggy moorland, and fog and mist may descend at any moment so a map and compass are recommended. At Anstey Common, an easier walk of just a few hundred yards down from the ridge road brings you to another stone, only 4ft 4in (1.3m) high, that stands in a similar position at the head of a narrow combe. Though in height less striking, its position immediately above the spring, running in the 'traditionally potent direction of south to north'

(Hazel Eardley-Wilmot, *Ancient Exmoor*) seems to make a statement to honour the divinity of springs and streams as the well-spring of life. Undoubtedly many stones have been lost, used for gateposts, rubbing stones and walling; at Longstone Wells farm, a stone which may be the one for which it is named was found beneath the slab floor and there are springs running underneath and nearby the house.

With many of Exmoor's monuments undoubtedly 'minilithic' rather than megalithic at less than 20in (0.5m) high, they are difficult to find and sadly all too vulnerable. It is thought that ten per cent were obliterated in the last century. At Withypool Hill is perhaps the best circle, about 40 small stones, only one of which stands as much as 2ft high, but it nevertheless has presence. Some 400 yards (365m) up the path from Portchester Bridge you have to deviate from the pathway and if you keep the heather line to your left you should stumble across it. Some 40 yards (36.5m) or so across and commanding the surrounding countryside, it is a shy and evocative survivor. One of the most accessible but least complete stone circles, at Porlock Common, was badly damaged in the Second World War.

Whereas the stones and much other evidence of man's presence on Exmoor are tantalisingly scant, even the most casual visitor would be hard-pressed to miss the great (and small) burial mounds and cairns that have seen generations come and go. We know of 370, varying in size from 2m to 35m in diameter, scattered pretty well all over Exmoor and it may be that there are more to be discovered. No problem with finding these, knitted as they are into the landscape. But it is worth taking the trouble to see them properly.

Following the sign for Five Barrows (named Five Burrows on the Ordnance Survey map and actually a group of nine), as you start up a gentle slope the barrows are not apparent. All of a sudden, after less than 200 yards (182m) or so exertion, they are there, the largest topped by its OS triangulation point, commanding one of those breathtaking panoramic 'roof of the world' views towards Hartland Point, Dartmoor and Bodmin Moor in the next county, with only

Part of the stone circle at Withypool, not spectacular but spiritual.

D. Coxon

the sound of silence and perhaps a passing crow. There is as much, if not more, spirituality to be felt here as at Stonehenge – and no car parks, visitor centres, fencing or indeed anything overtly twenty-first century (except a plume of factory 'smoke' far below in South Molton). One of those places where the essence of Exmoor hangs all around.

Our nearer ancestors assimilated their importance and put them to practical use as markers of boundaries, possibly as early as the thirteenth century, hence names such as Chapman Barrows, Wambarrows, Black Barrow and Alderman's Barrow. The latter, where four parish boundaries meet, was one of the bounds of Exmoor Forest since 1219 – known as Osmundesburg – and has undergone several name changes. Three quite large examples on Winsford Hill, the Wambarrows, also appear in the Exmoor Forest bounds since 1219 and 1279. Confusingly, the old English *beorg* from which barrow is thought to derive means mound so on Exmoor many natural mounds have barrow suffixes, such as Flexbarrow near Cow Castle.

The Longstone menhir with Long Stone barrow at Exmoor's ancient spiritual heart.

Wambarrows on Winsford Hill.

Again, relatively little archaeological work has been done to interpret Exmoor's barrows but we do know they are found in various settings – some stand alone, some in small groups; sometimes they are close to stone monuments, hut circles and field systems. There is a marked affinity with ridges and summits; they feature on all three of Exmoor's main east–west ridges and here are among the largest, such as Chapman Barrows. Chapman Barrows, comprising a highly unusual line of nine massive mounds, lies on the boundary of the parishes of Parracombe and Challacombe and is perhaps the most dramatic example with equally amazing views: to Dartmoor, the Welsh coast, Hartland Point, Lundy and, on a clear day, Bodmin Moor. Not too far away are Longstone Barrow and Wood Barrow both enjoying the same high point on the ridge and the same breathtaking views. Standing atop one of these spectacular and inevitably breezy high points, we can only speculate about the lives and beliefs of the people who put them there and why.

We know that the climate was better and that Exmoor was probably more populated then than either before or since, by people who, though not sophisticated, held religious beliefs and were no fools. But there is little other evidence to complete the jigsaw, partly because a lack of available stone meant houses would have been built of wood or turf that left no trace; partly because relatively little field work has been done.

Feats, forts and faeries

Quite suddenly, it seems, the age of our burial barrows ended, though the transition from the Bronze Age to the subsequent Iron Age was not as neat. Studies of pollen in peat deposits show a rapid decline in tree cover during the first millennium BC, the climate deteriorated and people moved to the fringes. Their most visible monuments are the seven hill-forts – and rather smaller hill-top enclosures. Their nature and siting seem to indicate a time of tribal warfare and unrest until the arrival of the Romans interrupted things but this may be misleading. Visible is also perhaps a misleading word. These are undoubtedly impressive earthworks – Shoulsbury Castle on the western fringe of the moor encloses 6 acres, commanding areas of landscape in a way that no prehistoric monuments had done before. But it is not what any young boy would recognise as a 'castle', with battlements and all, or even like the more elaborate hill-forts found elsewhere in southern England. Indeed some are so buried in woodland as to be virtually unrecognisable. It is now thought that as well as defensive strongholds they were places occupied by chieftains and the elite of society, and perhaps used for religious ritual.

Exmoor's hill-forts certainly exercise the minds of archaeologists because they vary so much in form and location. Similarly with the imagination of the visitor. Shoulsbury, occupying a lofty position looking out towards the Taw estuary and at 1500ft (450m) one of the highest hill-forts in England, is hidden from view on approach from the lane that flanks it and at time of writing is not accessible. Cow Castle, less than 3 miles (4.5k) away, conversely lies in the heart of former Royal Forest and is a favourite of many walkers: a tranquil, beautiful place but pretty wild and lonely. On a February day when the weather closed in suddenly it brought to mind the 'Poem of the Roman Soldier' (albeit referring to Hadrian's Wall):

Over the heather the wet wind blows
I've lice in my tunic and a cold in my nose.

Like Shoulsbury, it is thought unlikely that it was occupied permanently, but the folklore explanation for its presence is a much better tale anyhow. Situated on a low hill where a small stream called White Water meets the Barle, it is known to locals as Ring Castle, built by the pixies. The good pixies were constantly at war with the evil mine spirits who lived below ground but were no match for them. The Pixie Queen decided to build a mysterious and protective circle or castle on this conical hill, for which each stone or piece of turf used was imbued with the memory of a good deed that the pixies had done for the good of mankind. This created such a force of virtue that the evil mine spirits could not penetrate. It did not end there. As morning broke, rings of yellow smoke broke from the circle and gently floated away. Wherever they came to earth on Exmoor lush green circles were formed and it is within these faerie

Cold comfort at Cow Castle.

rings that the pixies dance in the moonlight, safe from the evil mine spirits. The walk to Cow Castle from either Simonsbath or just above Landacre Bridge is not too testing and a lovely and rewarding one.

It's probably as good a story as any for there has been little study of Exmoor's hill-forts. Wind Hill at Countisbury is the most formidable defensive earthwork on the moor – and perhaps the most impressive for the casual visitor – and could have held several families and their livestock, suggesting a high-status site or specialist function. Bat's Castle and Oldberry Castle might well have been occupied full time and, as focal points in the landscape, may have operated like trading posts. The former lies in the park of Dunster Castle and is quite elaborate, suggesting, along with its position in relation to other evidence of life at the time, that it was a seat of the élite of society and perhaps a sacred place designed to be seen at a distance. Along the Barle Valley from Oldberry Castle, Brewer's Castle and Mounsey Castle, named later for the ancient Monceaux family, now lie completely in woodland and the latter, though shrouded by vegetation appears to have survived completely intact. Again, much potential awaiting the time-teams.

Other smaller earthwork sites that bear the name of castle, like Roborough Castle near Lynton and Berry Castle, Porlock, are actually hill-slope enclosures, which to add to the confusion do not just occur on hill slopes. Dating is problematic and little is understood about them but archaeologists consider them to be the single most important area for research on Exmoor.

When the Romans finally pitched up in the first century AD, they mostly likely found people of the Dumnonii tribe which occupied Cornwall, Devon and much of West Somerset. But it seems there were no Boudica histrionics here and it is difficult to get a feeling for what their coming meant to Exmoor. Though Britain was a Roman colony for nearly four centuries, their tenure seems almost a blip, perversely heralding several hundred years when Exmoor's history seems to slip into the shadows.

Their most evocative sites are the two fortlets on the coast at Old Burrow and Martinhoe, occupying dramatic and spectacular clifftop positions, to watch over the Silures of South Wales. Finds of coins and pottery, both Roman and native, from these and other sites, point to trading with the 'conquerors' and Iron Age life carrying on much as before in the same settlement sites. (An interesting problem for local antiquarians was a penchant by the Rev. W.S. Halliday, builder of Glenthorne, for burying Roman coins in likely places, by way of a joke.) In some places like Spangate on the southern side of Dunkery and Sweetworthy on the northern side, archaeologists have found evidence that these pre-Roman sites were lived in and farmed right through until the nineteenth century.

We also know, and here finds are expanding that knowledge all the time, that the Romans were involved in iron mining and smelting, possibly for military use. As at Hawkcombe a 'dig' in 2004 promises to add still further to the picture. But Old Burrow was abandoned, probably because it was so exposed, and so too before long was Martinhoe, the whole episode over within thirty years, and once again the curtain drops on our knowledge of life on Exmoor, at least until Saxon times, but for one or two tiny mementoes.

Perhaps the most real and eloquent of all these people were those of the Bronze Age though, as Hazel Eardley-Wilmot points out, 'without art an ancient people are dumb to us'. In wondering what became of the Bronze Age moormen she argues a lovely case for them evading the incoming clumsy Celts by retreating to boggy hills and winding combes to in time become the good pixies of folklore. Perhaps another little bit of Exmoor magic, who knows? She continues:

> *The Bronze Age people have had so far the longest innings since Neolithic times. They farmed and hunted on these slopes, and looked out over these lovely sweeps of hill and sea. They were here until less than a hundred generations ago, and then quietly melted into the landscape.*

Who could put it better?

The ramparts of the hill-fort at Brewer's Castle are now well covered by woodland.

Chapter 5

A WILD ROMANCE

Like the ponies and deer, the appearance of the first primrose – truly the first rose – in the hedgebanks, woods, and field slopes is essentially Exmoor, harbinger of spring and and new life astir. Well, it is for those of us on the southern side of the moor, where the weather is more, well, Exmoor – wet, wet, wet; in the micro-climate of parts of the north-eastern side, and increasingly mild winters, they may be spotted as early as November. It is now quite common to see normally dormant animals such as bats and badgers active in such winters.

On the high moor, the best you can hope for is some golden glints of gorse as spring slumbers, while lower down the first signs arrive with the catkins of the hazel, and snowdrops. They carpet the floor of Snowdrop Valley as well as the roadside verges of Draper's Way. Then the profusions of primroses and sunny celandines jostle with violets, bluebells, orchids and more, in heart-stoppingly beautiful array. It seems that here, at least, all is right with the world. But, like the ponies and deer, they might have gone the same way as in many other parts of the country where they are never seen. They were nearly seen off by pesticide use on the hedgebanks, and from being picked or dug up by misguided admirers.

The humble 'common' primrose in some ways symbolises Exmoor's unique patchwork of habitats, where the rare and endangered co-

Truly the 'first rose', primroses light up the verges, banks and woodland as spring bursts forth.

exist with 'common' species, in total supporting an astonishing diversity of wildlife. Within the landscape of this smallest of our Parks are some 31 native mammals, including the red deer and Exmoor pony, over 243 species of bird, over 100 flowers and grasses and 1751 species of insects, including over 1000 moths. Clearly, you do not need to be a dedicated twitcher or tracker, to stand a high chance of seeing something – and often something quite rare and unusual – at almost any time of the year.

Snowdrop Valley is visited by thousands each spring.

You don't need to be too sharp-eyed to spot buzzard, now common in western and northern Britain, with more than one breeding pair per square mile of Exmoor. Soaring on the thermals, with up to 5ft wingspans, they are always a wonderful spectacle, even more so should you be lucky enough to see them locking talons and then falling to earth before starting again as part of their mating 'tango'.

Sadly, whilst Exmoor's moorland was off limits because of Foot and Mouth, the last red grouse quietly disappeared. Its demise, revealed by an RSPB survey in 2002, was not quite as significant as the extinction in the 1980s of its cousin, the black grouse or blackcock, which unlike the red was native to Exmoor. On the plus side, the Dartford warbler made its appearance, as did the yellowhammer, a bird the author hasn't seen since childhood. The warbler, a small dark elusive bird, is usually associated with gorse; when the males sing from the top of a bush to proclaim their territories is the best time to see its distinctive red eye, dark slate grey back and dull wine-red throat, breast and flanks.

More than 70 pairs of yellowhammers were recorded along the scrubby edges of the lower moorland. Whitethroats and stonechats also seemed to have benefited from the spread of gorse. The stonechat's pretty summer-visiting cousin, the whinchat, is thought to be more plentiful on Exmoor than anywhere in Britain, enjoying the heaths, scrubs and partly wooded valleys. Another gorse lover and winner is the linnet whose numbers have doubled, which is heartening as it is a species that has dramatically declined elsewhere.

A call of the wild noticeably silenced over the past few years has been the plaintive cry of the curlew, reduced to four pairs in the survey; the lapwing too appears to have gone from the high moor though it is not really understood why. Snipe are just about hanging on in there, as are merlin. The kestrel, though really a bird of the lowlands, is to be seen on the moor, as is its magnificent cousin the peregrine falcon, along with hobby, sparrowhawk, and in winter red kite, hen harrier and goshawk. The skylark too, though numbers have slumped by 20 per cent, thankfully can still be heard high above its moorland home.

Lunchtime for sparrowhawk – and he wasn't letting go!

42

Past and present forests

Despite the demise of Exmoor's original woodland, what survives has masses of interest and rare habitats to offer. Much of it is still relatively undisturbed ancient woodland – about as close as we come to natural in England, and of special interest in its own right – supporting a huge diversity of wildlife. Again we are lucky in being able to see much of it with little effort for much reward. For the rest of it, if you feel a little help is needed it is on hand, courtesy of the amazing variety of guided walks throughout the year run by the National Park Authority and by, among others, the photographer of this book.

In some woodland, ash and rowan predominate, while it is the western oakwoods for which Exmoor is most important internationally, dominated by small, crooked sessile oaks. Beech, though its presence seems now synonymous with Exmoor, is a relative newcomer. Though it has been in Britain since the Ice Age, there is not much peat-pollen evidence for it on Exmoor before Roman times, except perhaps on the southern edge of the moor in prehistoric times.

The hedgebanks, so definitive of Exmoor now, date only from the eighteenth century. Generally in Britain beech does not grow at the altitudes at which it is found here but landowners such as the Aclands, and later the Knights, favoured it because it was one of the few trees that would grow to maturity in moorland hedges, and when laid, dead leaves stayed on the trees through the winter, giving added windbreak. Birch Cleave Wood at Simonsbath, flanking the path to Cow Castle, is Britain's highest beech wood at 1200ft (300m) above sea level.

Whitebeam *(sorbus aria)*, from the Saxon word for tree, is less well-known owing to its very localised distribution, but has a special affinity with Exmoor, with no less than seven species to be found. The name derives from the silvery underside of the leaves which remains even in autumn when the leaves turn golden. Its red berries were once sold in markets and known locally as 'French hales' though in

Fiery red rowan reflects in Long Combe Water as it becomes Badgworthy Water.

Lancashire and Westmorland as chess-apples. Three species are found only on Exmoor, whilst another two are found only in South Wales and elsewhere in the West Country.

In the ancient woodland – so designated because it has existed for 400 years or more – a great number of plants are to be found. Much of Exmoor's woodland is now designated as Sites of Special Scientific Interest (SSSIs). A sense of antiquity and atmosphere exudes from the gnarled trunks, decorated with ferns, mosses and lichens. A large proportion of Britain's lichens are found on Exmoor, more than 350 all told and over 240 different species in woods around Dunkery. Horner has the honour of also being home to the extremely rare barbastelle and Bechstein bats. Again, Exmoor is probably one of the ricest bat habitats in the country with 14 out of the UK's 16 species already recorded. Beyond Horner the less rare horseshoe, pipistrelle, and noctule are well distributed. The species you are most likely to see is the pipistrelle and the commonest UK species, though in fact there are two types, defined by their echolocating frequencies, the common (45kHz) and the soprano at 55kHz! You can also see Devon's largest colony of lesser horseshoes in the Bat Cave at Arlington Court.

Fungus adds decorative detail to the woodland scene.

If you're not bats about bats, the more endearing though even less visible, dormouse is another lover of broadleaved woodland and Exmoor is a stronghold. The ancient woods of the Barle Valley between Withypool and Dulverton are particularly favoured by them though it seems they are turning up in all sorts of odd habitats from tussocks of purple moor-grass to the conifers of Croydon Forest. Unfortunately, this is unlikely to be an aspect of Exmoor to be discovered on a casual walk, unless exceedingly fortunate! The woodland is also home to fallow deer and roe deer, as well as red deer and hedgehogs. Woodpeckers, treecreepers and nuthatches all nest in holes in the trees, while wood warblers and pied flycatchers feast on insects in the oak canopy.

Oh so delicate, fleeting, but more possible to tick off in your *I-Spy* books (yes, they're still going!) are the handsome fritillary butterflies. Don't be deceived. Again Exmoor is a kind of time capsule for these handsome tawny orange and black-spotted insects, named for the spotted flowers they resemble. Seven of Britain's eight species still occur on Exmoor having virtually disappeared elsewhere thanks to intensive farming methods. The heath fritillary, Britain's rarest breeding butterfly, now extinct elsewhere and protected by law, has its main stronghold here. Feeding on common cow-wheat or plantain, it is found on woodland edges or the clearings associated with traditional coppices – hence their traditional name of 'woodman's followers' – a habitat that has vanished in many places. Spot them around heathland or wood edges in late June and July: Doone Country and around the flanks of Dunkery Hill are good places. The high brown, which is more spotted, has also suffered catastrophic decline, even here, with the disappearance of its habitats of mainly downland scrub, woods and copses. It feeds on bramble blossom, laying its eggs on the dog violet, and is now restricted to south-facing bracken slopes. The small pearl-bordered fritillary was common until the 1950s but has suffered a similar fate. Its caterpillar, too, feeds exclusively on violets in coppice, on bracken slopes and wet grassland. On Exmoor it is still a familiar sight over its bracken and wet grassland haunts in May and June but has lost numbers even here.

Moths are at home on the heathland, well over a thousand species making Exmoor their home. Many such as the emperor, oak eggar and beautiful yellow underwing, rely on the plants to be found here. The scarce blackneck is local to these parts; some are found in the Minehead area, others further afield.

The simply striking ermine moth.

Beetles are the largest known group of animals on earth, with 300,000 species – and they are the ones we know about! Like the moths, they number over a thousand species on Exmoor, from the familiar seven-spotted ladybird to the massive, but rarely seen, stag beetle which tends to hide away in tree stumps, gorging on grubs. It is perhaps all too easy to overlook the importance of insects like bees, wasps and ants which do vital work, pollinating crops and flowers. Hives are still taken onto the moor in late summer and the resulting honey has a distinctive light flavour. Though we think of the bees as common, in truth they are much less common, victims like the butterflies, of intensification of agriculture. Last but not least, a surprising subject to attract a government-decreed conservation

Illustration: Sheila Wilkinson

plan is the hornet robber fly, a fearsome-looking beast, but nevertheless endangered. The steep combes of the Exe and Barle valleys are one of the last refuges of this striking, large yellow-and-brown fly. Striking by nature, too, it ambushes its prey, grasshoppers and beetles, by stabbing them with a razor-sharp mouth blade. Perhaps not wildlife we would wish to seek out but still a part of Exmoor's intricate web of rare wildlife.

Coasts and rivers

Away from the high moor and woodland, on the coast, cliffs add value to Exmoor's diversity of habitats. England's highest cliffs are home to nesting birds like the guillemot, razorbill, kittiwake, and ravens, as well as the rare peregrine falcon. Here where the natural woodland descends almost to the beach are sessile oak, yew and the rare whitebeams. Around the saltmarsh behind Porlock's shingle ridge it is worth looking out for curlew and oyster-catchers as well as unusual plants such as seablite and glasswort.

If walking near one of the streams and rivers, stretching to 300 miles (483km) as they flow off Exmoor, you should be lucky enough to spot anything from the delightful dippers bobbing in and out of the water, and grey wagtails, heron, perhaps a flash of kingfisher, dragonflies and water insects. In the clear water are brown trout and loaches, as well as salmon. On the bankside Exmoor is one of the main places to find Irish spurge and Cornish moneywort which like shady stream banks.

Dipper.

Where the Exe and Barle meet at Black Pool.

The otter, now immortalised wherever the Tarka name appears on the moor, was threatened with extinction because of river pollution and clearance of river banks. But thankfully special conservation measures since it was declared an endangered species in the 1970s have seen it make a comeback. You would be very lucky to see one in the wild, being mainly nocturnal and wary of humans, but might spot their five-toed prints in the mud. Their droppings, known as spraints, which mark territory, might be another clue but are small and easy to miss.

The fields and hedgerows surrounding farm land are important habitats in their own right, for small mammals like badger, fox, hares, moles and rabbits. Barns and outbuildings provide homes for bats and owl, indeed the ghostly barn owl has made something of a comeback. Little owls, which can often be seen during the day, are found in the lowland eastern area, while the most common tawny owl, with its familiar toowhit-twhoo call, is likely to be heard over a wide area. Short eared owls are mainly winter visitors and can be seen hunting by day; their long-eared cousins are nocturnal and less vocal so more secretive.

The beauty of it is that though we may be aware of the dedicated work and care behind the scenes to 'manage' and conserve wildlife,

the visible result is that each venture onto the moor, along the coast or through woodland will present fresh 'life-in-the-raw' experiences, possibly fleeting, but nonetheless exciting. On a walk to see the standing stone on West Anstey Common, there was the beauty of ponies, a glimpsed merlin – rare, yes, but that wing shape was etched on the sky – a fox loping along a ridge, and a snatched glimpse of, was that a brambling or whinchat? One day near Five Barrows the author was astonished to see a heron fly gracefully up from a high-altitude drink.

On another occasion, driving down one of those narrow lanes where grass grows quaintly down the middle, a tawny owl was sitting quite serenely in the middle of the road. You can spot your wildlife in amazing places on Exmoor!

Wild goat in the Valley of Rocks.

Wild poppy.

Not loved by all but this fox has Exmoor to roam rather than just suburbia.

INTO THE LIGHT

Nowhere were the so-called Dark Ages that followed the Romans' withdrawal in AD410 more murky than in the mists of Exmoor. But for three inscribed monuments – the Caratacus stone on Winsford Hill, the Culbone stone and the Cavadus stone – which tell us very little in themselves, there is practically nothing left of the period. With hardly any archaeological clues, or evidence of where people lived, we have only general historical information about the whole South West, and pointers from place-names and early church dedications.

In the Kingdom of Dumnonia the Celtic way of life seems to have carried on as it had for centuries; there was a significant migration of people from Devon and Cornwall to Armorica – hence its change of name to Brittany, reflecting their origins – and the Anglo-Saxons were advancing across Britain. But how it all affected Exmoor, and how much it related to the Exmoor that

The enigmatic Culbone Stone.

took shape from Norman times – that we can recognise today – is really not known.

Place-names, church dedications and a scatter of words still in use do offer clues. Several Exmoor churches are dedicated to early Christian saints, as in Wales and Brittany: Beuno at Culbone, St Petrock, Brendon after the Irish saint, Brendan, and Dubricius at Porlock. These were missionaries and dignitaries of the fifth and sixth centuries, and though the dedications were not made until some 500 years later, they may have perpetuated earlier ecclesiastical foundations. The word combe for valley is obviously similar to the Welsh cwm; Minehead comes from *mynydd*, meaning a large hill, and the sinister sounding Hangman Hills, more prosaically come from *maen*, meaning a stony hill or cairn. According to J.Ll.W. Page in *An Exploration of Exmoor*, even the *ex* of Exmoor is partly Celtic, deriving from *osc* or *uisg* for water.

Mists of history.

Culbone church – dedicated to St Beuno, a Welsh saint of the sixth or seventh century. Originally named Chetenore or Kitnor, the parish became Culbone, perhaps from Kil Beuno – church or cell of St Beuno.

But it was not until around AD700, forty-two years after the defeat of the Celts at Penselwood in Somerset in AD658, that the Saxons made their bid for Exmoor, ironically signalling an end to its exile from history. It is their names for farms and villages that are still very present today. It is presumed they met little resistance as there were no important battles and we have no evidence of the Iron Age forts being used again. It seems that some fled and established new settlements on the fringes of the moor; Charles, High Bray and Molland all derive from Celtic names but one wonders why they were safe here, when the Saxons were intent on grabbing the best land. One of the few Celtic connection place-names is thought to be Countisbury.

The Saxons cut across the middle of the moor using the Harepath – a Saxon word meaning army road – one of the most ancient trackways in Britain and a major trade route that ran from the Midlands through to Cornwall. The path that follows its moorland route, from Mole's Chamber running north-east to meet the Challacombe road, today still illustrates how it would have enabled them to dominate the uplands, using it to move supplies and make surprise attacks on any settlements still holding out.

Though the Saxons left little else to show for their 350-year stay, and would be themselves subsumed by the Normans, most of Exmoor's villages date to these times. Place names ending in 'ton' are evidence of such villages, as are names such as Oare (*Are*), Stoke Pero (*Stocke*), Horner (*Hernola*), Cornham (*Quarnham*) and Winsford (*Winesford*). *Cott* and *wyrth*, meaning smaller, low-status settlements, come from this period; *wud, bearu, graf, hyrst* and *holt* all have woodland connotations. *Hiwisc* – now huish – refers to one hide unit, probably the holding of a free peasant. A 'barton' was a large family farm, originally meaning 'barley-farm' ie one that was good for corn, whether barley or wheat, and as such usually the lord's farm.

Though place-names indicate that some of the more intrepid might have settled on the uplands, most, unsurprisingly, favoured the better land of the fringes of the moor. They cleared woodland and grew corn and other crops in small fields which they protected from the elements with high wide banks. They also began the practice in summer of driving cattle and sheep up to the higher pastures, bringing them down to winter on the farms, a custom that would endure, and still does, for over 1000 years. In time the Saxon kings started to appropriate land not in use for farming and as such often unsuitable 'wasteland'. These became the king's deer and game reserves – later the Royal Forests – which would dominate Exmoor's fortunes for nigh on 1000 years.

At first the events that would eventually culminate in William the Conqueror's victory and the end of the old Saxon order, hardly touched Exmoor. All appears to have been peaceful, at least until AD878 when a Viking brother of Ivar the Boneless and Halfdan landed with 23 ships at a place the *Anglo-Saxon Chronicle* tells us was Arx Cynuit, which some argue was Countisbury, where the great earthwork on Wind Hill would have made an ideal fortress defence. Archaeologists are not so convinced and have found no evidence of its re-use – Northam has also been mooted as the site – but wherever it was, the victory was decisive, with the nameless Viking and more than 800 men of his men killed. Subsequent piratical Viking visitors were repelled over the next century, and King Alfred defeated the 'Great Army' of the Danes to save Wessex in AD 878, but by 1016 the invaders and King Canute were in charge.

In 1052 the rumblings and power struggles that marked the end of Edward the Confessor's long reign brought the then outlawed Harold, the future king, to Porlock, with disastrous consequences for the tiny port. Harold and his father Earl Godwin had been dispossessed by Leofric, Earl of Mercia, whose son Algar held Porlock. Intent on revenge Harold and his army, raised in Ireland, landed at Porlock where they killed many men, looted, then set fire to the town, destroying it and reputedly the palace of a Saxon king. On Godwin's death Harold became an earl and later king; nine months later he was slain at the Battle of Hastings or Senlac and any last remnants of Saxon dominance were at an end.

But their legacy, as we have seen, certainly lived on. Devon and Somerset existed as shires as early as the eighth and ninth centuries (Hoskins 1992; Dunning 1987) and their system of parochial organisation, begun in the late Saxon period, was formalised in the eleventh and twelfth centuries. The Domesday Book of 1086, ironically, paints a vivid picture of life on Exmoor as the Normans found it – though of course lands and property that had belonged to the Saxons automatically now passed to the Conqueror and his barons. It lists the manors or 'home farms', the status of those who lived there, land use and stock – as well as making special mention of the wild ponies of the moor. We see the hamlets and farms of the Brendon Hills, names such as Huish, Leigh Barton and Woodadvent, and villages such as Treborough and Rodhuish. We learn of Stoke Pero having land for two ploughs, 50 acres of pasture and 60 acres of woodland, and of 'Alric' who farmed at around 400m at Radworthy, below the Chapman Barrows, though his land would be given to William de Pollei.

All this reflected how countryside settlements, however scattered, had settled into a manorial pattern established by the Saxons, that of the manor or home farm, barton or country estate, with its related farmsteads and land, that would continue to be the pivot upon which country life turned until the concept of parish was evolved, but continuing far beyond. At the heart of it all on Exmoor, for the next few centuries, was the Royal Forest.

The Harepath at Mole's Chamber, an ancient trackway probably dating to Bronze Age times.

Three mysterious stones

Culbone stone – Buried in dense woodland near Culbone Church is a curious stone with a strange inscription of a tilted wheeled cross. It was found somewhere around 1940 lying face downwards and re-erected close to the same spot. The stone has been likened to other inscribed stones of the sixth or seventh century but these occur on Lundy, South Wales, Cornwall and Brittany and hardly anywhere else in southern England. It lies near a stone row and close to an ancient ridgeway from Lynmouth to Porlock so may be a pagan Iron Age motif, as indicated by an extended line of the cross beyond the circle which appears to have been added at a later date – possibly to 'Christianise' the stone. The parish boundary follows the stone row almost exactly and it seems likely that this too was another way in which pagan monuments were incorporated into Christianity.

The **Caratacus** or Caractacus stone near Spire Cross on Winsford Hill bears the inscription *Caraaci Nepus* – which is usually translated to mean kinsman of Caratacus, a British rebel of the first century AD, but the inscription is almost certainly fifth or sixth century. Because it stands near a former ridgeway, the stone may well be older than its inscription, presumably placed so that it could be seen by passers-by. In the thirteenth century it is recorded as the Langeston, a Forest boundary mark. After being vandalised in 1923, it was reset under a shelter.

Cavadus stone – This stone, inscribed *Cavdi Filius Civili* meaning Cavadus son of Civilis, is definitely not in its original location and stands in a private garden near Lynton. Like the Caratacus Stone, the inscription is fifth or sixth-century Latin, not Celtic, and the style is typical of the fifth century.

Caratacus Stone on Winsford Hill.

Chapter 7

THE ROYAL FOREST

The term Royal Forest conjures up vivid medieval pictures of brightly-clad kings and noblemen pursuing red deer and other game through rich green woodland and flower-strewn glades. Something of a misnomer. The word *forest* originally meant outland – even down to Shakespeare's time – land beyond even that considered as waste land, which through Saxon times was gradually claimed as rights of common, where cottagers grazed their few cows or pigs and cut furze and peat. The unclaimed land came to be regarded as royal property, where deer and other wild animals were reserved for the king, and once the Normans arrived, subject to increasingly oppressive forest laws.

The Domesday survey records three Saxons – Dodo, Almar and Godric (now there's a name for a boy band!) – holding land above

Antlers shed in the grass – symbolic of Exmoor from the days of the Royal Forest through to the present National Park.

Withypool until King Edward's death, and describes them as *forestarii*. The Conqueror rapidly relieved them of their land and duties, but this seems to indicate that Exmoor was already a hunting forest. In fact, of the 70 or so royal forests claimed by the Normans, Exmoor had a huge disadvantage in that it had few trees and thus few places where the deer could harbour at its heart, and this led to the bounds – and the harsh laws that ruled within them – being brutally extended.

All the adjacent land, and sometimes beyond, was appropriated or 'afforested' by being declared 'purlieu', a Norman concept that brought dire consequences on any man or beast falling foul of the laws protecting the king's deer and game. Anyone caught illegally killing or in any way interfering with these, or even the greenery on which they fed, was liable to the death penalty, or perhaps a lesser

The treeless view up Hoccombe Water towards Brendon Two Gates illustrates clearly the earlier different meaning of forest.

Exmoor's red deer – hunted from the mists of time but ultimate survivors.

sentence such as mutilation, a long period rotting in jail, banishment or blinding! All dogs capable of hunting them and living within the new boundaries were deliberately lamed by cutting off three toes of the forefoot. Incredibly, there is no record of any king ever actually hunting on Exmoor, though it begs the question why King John, a fervent hunter, should have busied himself grabbing vast tracts of land, unless for his own use. Certainly, the king's nobles, such as the de Mohuns of Dunster and Roger la Zuche of North Molton, and other passing persons of high rank, were allowed to kill deer and records show that they did. But, with poaching rife, there was extra profit to be had from fines and extortion, and income from the summer grazing.

Whether any king visited or not, at the beginning of the twelfth century a huge part of Exmoor was under Royal Forest rule: the parishes of Hawkridge, Withypool, Exmoor Forest, Oare, Culbone, Porlock, Luccombe, Stoke Pero, Cutcombe, Exford, Winsford, and Dulverton with parts of Selworthy, Wootton Courtenay and Exton. If things seemed bad under the Conqueror they were now a whole lot worse. While Henry II was gifting charters to towns, times were

miserable in the outlands He and his sons Richard and John annexed more and more lands and strengthened the savage decrees, until the population could take no more. In 1204 the men of Devon paid 100 marks to King John (about £666) to be disafforested. This released land on the Devon side of Exmoor, and similar land around the Forest of Dartmoor.

When in 1215 both Normans and English rose against John, forcing him to sign the Magna Carta at Runnymede, all these recent land grabs were annulled, the boundaries to be as at Henry II's coronation: but it resolved little if anything. Only John's seizures, not those of his father and brother, were disafforested at once. It was not until after his death that the young Henry III attempted to put things right, by ordering a new perambulation of the bounds and declaring, 'Henceforth, let no man lose life or members for our venison.' Another king who did not live up to his promises: it was to be nearly another 200 years of protests, petitions and royal shenanigans before this 300-year-old episode of tyranny lost its grip and the old boundaries of the Forest were more or less restored.

From this time, c.1400, the Forest was a central portion of unenclosed land surrounded by the commons of the parishes beyond, 20,344 acres and two perches, equivalent to the present-day parish of Exmoor. Its boundaries in these times were invisible (a feature much appreciated by poachers), defined only by where they met the commons' edges and acknowledged landmarks, reinforced every few years when foresters and farmers 'perambulated' the Forest, while each spring neighbouring parishes 'beat the bounds'.

Though this area remained uninhabited until the seventeenth century, the upholding of its laws and organisation of grazing rights influenced life far beyond it profoundly. Sadly, it is impossible here to more than sketch in an idea of the colourful, vibrant and no doubt frequently harsh way of life that was lived by the good men and women (and bad) of medieval Exmoor. Chaucer, who had strong connections with the area and may well have visited, would certainly

From the top of Challacombe Hill looking towards Woodbarrow Gate from Roostitchen – the old Forest boundary.

have found similar inimitable characters to those of his *Canterbury Tales*. He summed it up: 'The web of our life is a tangled yarn, good and ill together.'

The most important official for the next few centuries was the Warden of the Forest, charged with protecting the king's deer and game, and looking after the land in return for grazing rights, sheep being the main source of revenue. In such a male-dominated world, it is interesting to see that this largely hereditary role was for a time held by a woman, Sabina Pecche, who inherited the title from her brother Richard de Plessy. But little is known about her and that's a discovery to be kept for another day. Only one other woman held the office, Margaret Boevey, some 400 years later.

There were also Foresters, who saw to the day-to-day running of the Forest; Verderers who maintained law and order and dealt with minor disputes; Regarders, who inspected and reported on the state of the Forest; and Agisters who counted the stock. Such titles are still in use in the New Forest today. They must have been tense and dangerous times, as a good few country folk played cat and mouse with the king's men, poaching, clearing land, cutting peat and stubbornly refusing to melt back to the margins. Even the parsons of Hawkridge and Oare are on record as conniving, according to records of the supreme court, the Eyre, the former being detained in prison though he was later 'pardoned for the sake of the King's soul'. The Eyre, which was held away from Exmoor, gave way from around the end of the thirteenth century, to a court of 'inquisition' or trial by jury called the Swainmote Courts, held, though it is hard to imagine now, at the present-day beauty spot of Landacre Bridge, then a fortnight later at Hawkridge churchyard. Hawkridge at this time took precedence over Withypool and had the parish church.

From all the wranglings and challenges over boundaries and rights, had gradually emerged a system, with the Swainmote Court at its heart, that involved various players other than the king's men: Free Tenants, Suitors at Large and Free Suitors. It may be that the latter

Landacre Bridge – hard to imagine this favourite picnic spot as the scene of the Swainmote Courts.

dated back to the days of the Saxons, Dodo, Almar and Godric, who held Withypool and Hawkridge in return for Forest duties, the tradition continuing after they had relinquished the land. At some stage 52 tenants of Withypool and Hawkridge were made Free Suitors, so that they held their farms and rights of pasturage, turbary and fish, in exchange for carrying out the Forest duties. These included attending the Swainmote Courts and driving the Forest nine times a year on horseback, for horses and cattle and once a year for sheep.

The Suitors at Large, appropriately, represented the other townships and manors (later to be the parishes) around Exmoor, who were supposed to attend the Swainmote, though often their bailiff would be sent, and maintain the boundary stones, again in exchange for pasturage. Thus the business of taking sheep, principally, but also cattle and horses up onto the moor and back, twice a year – for the sheep which were brought down again for shearing – must have dominated a large part of everyday life for most of the population. One estimate of the numbers towards the end of the sixteenth century reckons that some 40,000 sheep, 1000 rother (horned) cattle and 400 'horse' beasts (ponies), went for summer grazing. The custom of 'Crying the Moor' came about as each spring men were

Hawkridge churchyard, scene of the Swainmote Court.

Stone tomb lid in Hawkridge church bearing a French and Latin inscription, possibly of William de Plessy who died in 1274.

sent to the market towns around the moor, to proclaim the rates for taking in different animals. It is still quoted that even in these hard times for sheep farmers, there are still more sheep than people in North Molton parish. Then, as testified by the village's unusually large church with its 90 foot tower, wool was wealth. En route to their pastures, these valuable beasts were counted on, then counted off again at shearing time at strategically placed Telling Houses. Any unshorn sheep were impounded in the Forest pound, south of the river at Withypool, another being built later at Simonsbath. Once shorn the sheep were counted back and again in October when they they were returned to their farms for the winter. The cattle drifts occurred two or three times a year, five times a year for the ponies.

How many Telling Houses there were is not recorded and none are left standing. Yarde Down and Mole's Chamber are the most likely sites but inaccurate mapping in the past and lack of tangible evidence leave us little the wiser. So, with only the odd boundary stone, and the continuing presence of sheep, cattle and ponies, and all now quiet at Landacre Bridge, much imagination is needed to picture a time that must have been an unpredictable blend of turbulence and tradition. We can see more evidence of Bronze Age man and woman than of this time in Exmoor's history though there are written sources.

The single farm and hamlets that are still the most common type of settlement on Exmoor also offer an enduring link with an earlier pattern of occupation. Through the centuries, from those Saxon beginnings, farming and the settlements that grew up around it had become established as the mainstay of Exmoor life. The thirteenth century saw the population expand, more land taken into cultivation and prosperity. As the land was split between heirs, barton farms expanded adding smaller farms to form hamlets or outlying farms. But in 1348 came the Black Death, wiping out more than half of Britain's population, and the beginning of the end of the old manorial system with much of its labour pool dead and buried. It must have had some impact on Exmoor though again, to what degree, seems unclear. It is thought unlikely that desertion of villages such as Badgworthy was solely caused by it, but rather the result of a combination of factors – deteriorating climate and better land becoming available through death elsewhere.

It seems that for the next century and a half things carried on in and around the Forest much as before until 1504 when the winds of change again blew over Exmoor. The austere Henry VII, who was little interested in hunting and keen to increase his revenues, leased the Forest to Sir Edmund Carew for a rent of £46.13s.4d, a figure that remained unchanged until the last lease was given up in 1814, and the beginning of the end of the Royal Forest. The Swainmote Courts still met and we are told that even as the English Civil War tore the rest of the countryside asunder, Exmoor, as S.H. Burton puts it, remained 'a little kingdom and the Warden was its ruler'. It is difficult to know on the sparse evidence available. Well maybe. Certainly there were skirmishes; in 1642 the Luttrells of Dunster Castle sent Royalist forces packing, to make their escape across the heart of the moor; two years later the king's men were back, and Barnstaple for a time fell into the hands of the Royalists. At Combe

Sydenham most of the traditional E-shape of the Elizabethan-style manor house was lost, and wrens still fly in through bullet-holes left in the front door by the Roundheads as they passed through.

With the execution of Charles I, Parliament made haste to dispose of 'the Honours, Manors and lands heretofore belonging to the late King, Queen and Prince' and though the Forests were excluded from the Act, Exmoor, having been leased since Carew's day, was considered a Chase and was included. The purchaser – James Boevey, a wealthy merchant of Dutch ancestry – was to be almost a one-man civil war in himself. From a date carved in a beam, it can be assumed that he immediately set about building in 1653 a rather fine house at Simonsbath, at the heart of the Forest – its first dwelling, now Simonsbath House Hotel, and the first farm. With typical energy he set about the enclosing and improvement of his land land and within a year was at loggerheads with the locals. John Aubrey in *Brief Lives*, called him:

> … a person of great temperance and deepe thoughts … a great lover of Natural Philosophie. His whole life has been perplexed in humane affairs, in which he alwaies overcame. He had many law-suites and powerfull adversaries; one lasted eighteen years …

Boevey also wrote 32 works 'mostly philosphical' which included *The Art of Governing the Tongue* and the *Art of Gaining Wealth*, but in practice was to spend much of the next forty-three years – the longest tenure of any Warden – being a thorn in the side for Exmoor's 'good husbandmen' as MacDermot puts it in *A History of the Forest of Exmoor*. In short (the tale being told in full by MacDermot), he acted much like the kings who so many centuries before had attempted to ride roughshod over the rights of ancient neighbours; hiking up grazing rates and bringing endless lawsuits against them. Despite the land having reverted to the Crown at the Restoration in 1660 – which he neatly got round by becoming the lessee – he brought yet another lawsuit against 17 farmers over pasturing whilst also being embroiled in litigation over his first wife's property in Holland. Here he found

All roads seem to lead to Simonsbath, where James Boevey created the first dwelling in the former Royal Forest. His fine house is on the left of the picture.

himself languishing in jail for some years, which must have seemed welcome respite to those on Exmoor, but it was not to last. On his return yet another claim was lodged against the farmers for unpaid dues. Then in 1675 came his most audacious move yet, laying claim to the commons of all the bordering parishes. The man who 'alwaies overcame' did not ; in 1679 he lost the case and from then on seems, wisely at last, to have retired to Cheam in Surrey, leaving the day-to-day running of the estate to his Deputy Forester, Henry Smith. Even then he apparently did not lose his appetite for litigation – there can have been little sorrow on Exmoor when in 1696 he died.

His widow, Margaret, became the second woman to be Warden but she sold the remainder of her lease to Robert Siderfin eight years later, and the 'good husbandmen' must have raised quite a cheer. It has left many a historian speculating as to what drove Boevey. Did he set out with dreams of creating a great estate, see a chance to make his fortune, or see in his fine but lonely new home a place to improve his rather erratic health and write his books? He built his house and farm and a new Forest pound, put Simonsbath on the map and created it the new administrative 'capital' of the moor and planted a new Hoar Oak tree to replace the ancient boundary marker that had fallen in 1658. Oh, and he was in charge at the time when R.D. Blackmore set his romance *Lorna Doone*. Now his house remains and his name graces a rather good tearoom/restaurant. No doubt if he came back today, he would probably sue.

Chapter 8

OLD AND NEW

The era of the Royal Forest was inexorably drawing to a close but there would still be Wardens of illustrious cut whose legacy is still with us today in the shape of the red deer, Exmoor's hunting tradition and the preservation of the ponies.

Showing a similar turn in fancy footwork to Boevey, Robert Walpole's son, the second Lord Orford, had married Margaret, the daughter and heiress of Samuel Rolle of Heanton Satchville in 1724 – bringing along with her the great Rolle estates and a fine pack of staghounds. Calling on his contacts as the prime minister's son, Lord Orford managed to obtain a lease of the Forest, perfect hunting territory, for nothing. His good fortune also meant a revival of interest in the deer, which had declined with previous Wardens, and hunting on a regular basis was resumed for the first time in over a hundred years. Orford unfortunately found himself dispatched to a happier hunting ground within a year, leaving two leases to his son. Perhaps the third Lord Orford disliked hunting or perhaps he had a good eye for a profit, because he left the hunting of his deer to Sir Thomas Acland of Holnicote and eventually sold the remaining twenty-eight years of his three leases (having added another) to Sir Thomas for a handsome £4200.

With Sir Thomas in the saddle, to be followed by another two Sir Thomases – hailing from one of the oldest families in Devon and Somerset – came a remarkable chapter in Exmoor's history that is still writ large in many ways, though the Aclands relinquished their lands and influence long since. With their country seat at Holnicote on the north-eastern edge of the moor, and other property around Exmoor, they brought a natural empathy to the custom and practice of the Forest; in their time the three Sir Ts restored the Forest and the office of Warden to something of their former glory.

The first Sir Thomas had astutely married Elizabeth Dyke of Tetton, who brought to the deal the Holnicote estate and more. But before he was thirty, she died and Sir Thomas threw himself obsessively into the life of a country squire, spending the entire hunting season either at his Pixton estate or Holnicote. It was open house at both throughout the season and the hospitality was legendary. He followed his wife's uncle as Master of Staghounds – holding the position for thirty years – and set up the first pack of stag hounds to be kennelled on the moor. When he settled Pixton on his eldest son, Holnicote became his hunting lodge. Contrary to a popular view, usually held by outsiders, the hunting revival afforded protection to the deer, which had declined rapidly at the hands of poachers. Owning much of central Exmoor, he boasted that he could ride 30 miles from Killerton to Holnicote on his own land.

Tragedy struck again when his eldest son died, aged just thirty-four, closely followed in 1779 by Holnicote being destroyed by fire, along with all his hunting trophies and collection of stags' heads. One small consolation was that the Exeter Cup, won in 1774 by his beloved horse Grecian at the Haddon races, survived, but little else. After a brief return as Master, with Major Bassett, he died in 1785, aged just sixty-three.

His title passed to his youngest son, the second Sir Thomas, who having raced through much of his inheritance, made good by marrying Henrietta Hoare of the banking family, who produced two sons and two daughters during the nine short years of their marriage. Though he had been reputedly estranged from his father – probably because of his profligacy – he shared the same tastes and was likewise known as 'Sir Thomas his Honour' (causing confusion in hunting annals), was an illustrious huntsman and Master of Foxhounds. He favoured Holnicote, now rebuilt, as his home over the family's Killerton estate in mid Devon, and had even replaced his father's collection of stags' heads with 101 of his own. Unlike his father, hunting was his whole life and Holnicote his main home, but again the curse struck. Aged forty-two, he was taken ill unexpectedly and died.

Once again a young boy inherited the estates, the seven-year-old third Sir Thomas, who being of a less bucolic, more thinking turn of mind, revived a family tradition of wider philanthropy and standing for Parliament, which he entered in 1812. He is credited with saving the Exmoor pony which, like the deer, had suffered mixed fortunes. He took 400 ponies from the Forest to set up the core herd on Winsford Hill, today known as the Anchor herd from his anchor-shaped brand.

In 1810 Sir Thomas applied for renewal of the lease of the Royal Forest, which was due to expire in 1814, and then applied to buy the freehold but once again the winds of change were blowing. Timber was needed for the Navy and somehow Exmoor came into the frame as land where oak could be grown. It seems the city's grasp on country matters changes little. Surveyors were duly dispatched, options drawn up but their reports significantly made no mention of the Hoar Oak Tree. It seems they just did not check and consequently did not realise that it was hardly country for raising oaks. Nevertheless the Crown pressed ahead, apportioning, in 1815, 10,262 acres, and allocating other land to Acland, Sir Charles Bampfylde of North Molton, and others. As ever, the little man and rights going back centuries lost out. Suddenly, and perhaps persuaded by Sir Thomas of the futility of the oak-growing plan, the Government put the Forest up for sale. It was snapped up by a man from the Midlands for £50,000, eclipsing offers by Acland and Lord Fortescue. The Forest and all its ways, good and bad, were about to change for ever.

The Great Sir Thomas, as the third Sir Thomas came to be known, gained a reputation as a fearless campaigner against injustices such as slavery and conditions in the cotton mills, and had a long and happy marriage, resulting in 21 grandchildren. But the tragedy that seemed to dog the family was never far way. When an epidemic of scarlet fever killed his daughter-in-law and one of his grandchildren, it was to Holnicote that his son Tom and five remaining children fled. For the second time in its history, the thatched house burned down. This Tom was also a man of great integrity and moral courage; he instigated agricultural reform and was largely instrumental in the founding of the Bath and West Society and its annual show; he also had a great impact on the development of state education. Curiously, he loved to sketch but preferred to do so on his many travels away from Exmoor. After the fire he often returned to stay with his lifelong mentor the Revd Joshua Stevenson, now past his fiftieth year as parson at Selworthy, and would visit the school and pensioners' cottages on Selworthy Green. He kept up his habit of walking up the hill after church on Sunday, a practice commemorated by a stone shelter at the head of Selworthy Combe.

In 1917 Charles Acland, who keeping up a 150-year tradition of Sir Thomases opted to be known as Sir Thomas the Twelfth, made the

Selworthy Green, largely created by the Aclands on their Holnicote estate.

dramatic decision to hand his Holnicote and Killerton estates to the National Trust on a 500-year lease. In 1944, 15th Baronet Sir Richard, another man of high principles and political ideals, gave the Holnicote estate's 12,443 acres to the National Trust. It included Dunkery Beacon and Selworthy – claimed by many to be the most beautiful village in England – which had been enlarged and partly recreated as a model village by the Great Sir Thomas.

Around the large hillside church and existing few cottages, the enlightened Sir Thomas created the chocolate-box village we see today 'as a refuge for estate pensioners', and oversaw the planting of well over a million exotic and native trees on the slopes of the hills. The National Trust's protection of the estate, which holds much of Exmoor's most characteristic scenery, architecture and wildlife, was a major factor in Exmoor becoming a National Park so, as his ancestor had been the saviour of the ponies, Sir Richard too was a saviour of Exmoor.

The Knights

When the axe fell for good on the Royal Forest, a thousand-year chapter of Exmoor's history closed and another opened; the next players, and their epic struggle, was nineteenth-century soap opera. On the face of it, it was a classic case of new money and old – the Knight fortune having been made in the Midlands iron industry – but theirs was courageous, enterprising and surprisingly cultured stock with dynastic dreams of their own. John Knight genuinely relished the challenge of making this 'desert bloom', in tune with the new age of agricultural progress but he would find the barren wilderness tough to tame; in the end Exmoor broke him.

He was now owner of the former Royal Forest, with mineral rights – thought to be worth nothing – thrown in. Within two years, in true Monopoly-board style, he bought Boevey's farm, the sizeable tracts allotted to Acland and Sir Charles Bampfylde, along with their mineral rights, various smaller allotments and the manor of Brendon, increasing his holding by half again. The terms of sale meant that he had to enclose the former Forest and by 1824 the formidable task of

building a wall along the 30-mile circumference was complete, whilst new roads replaced the old rough tracks from Simonsbath to Exford, North and South Molton and Brendon and Lynton.

Like the Bronze Age relics the wall does fire the imagination. Probably anyone who has visited Exmoor will recall their surprise on following the signs to Simonsbath, which seems to offer promise of a town at least, to find so little there. Stretches of the wall that survive, like the section that snakes alongside the walker from Simonsbath to Cow Castle and Landacre, set you to wondering where all the stone came from, and of the lives of the labourers who made it and the roads. Knight ignored advice to create a village at Simonsbath and preferred to employ only unmarried men who lodged in makeshift dormitories in the farm outbuildings. Others lodged at Exford, a good 5 or 6 miles away, which benefited instead. One story goes that the men of Brendon demolished after dark what had been built in the day in protest at their share of the allotments going to the Suitors at Large but their efforts in their own small area did not delay things much overall.

John Knight's wall to enclose the former Royal Forest snakes through the moor, here by Hoccombe Water – an amazing feat, considering the lack of available stone and labour.

Knight then set about improving the land, a challenge he had already successfully met in his home county. He was inspired by the work of the likes of Coke of Norfolk who had transformed English agriculture with new methods, seed and mechanical equipment, to meet the growing need for food for a rapidly growing industrial population. He started by clearing the land in the traditional local way, by burning, turning the soil and liming to sweeten the soil, which was sound enough practice. But the acid soils of Exmoor needed vast quantities of expensive lime and despite all the undoubted energy and skill he brought to the quest, it was doomed by his fatal and enduring mistake – growing corn by the four-course crop rotation method – could never work under upland Exmoor skies. Occasionally good luck did produce a decent harvest, which only blinkered him further and he determinedly ploughed the same furrow for some twenty years until 1841 before handing the management reins to his son Frederic.

His attempts at introducing new stock also suffered mixed fortunes. He travelled the length and breadth of the country to introduce quality breeds: Hereford and West Highland cattle, Westphalian pigs, Arab horses to run with the native ponies and great herds of Cheviot sheep, as well as Merinos, alongside the native Horns. Again the weather won. The 'improved' breed of pony could not winter on the moor, nor could the cattle, and with so many sheep on the moor, it was a rustler's paradise. The Irish guards he employed spent so much time fighting among themselves, they added to the problem.

Pinkworthy Pond – variously spelt Pinkery, as it is pronounced – along with its so-called canal, was another Knight white elephant, and enigma. No one really knows why he brought in 200 Irish labourers specially to work on the project which involved damming the infant River Barle just south of where it rises on the desolate Chains. The 'pond' is actually a lake of about 7 acres and the 'canal' is more by way of a ditch, not linked to the lake. Knight intended to build a railway from Simonsbath to Porlock Weir and perhaps Pinkworthy was to supply the necessary water power for raising

Above: *Many have puzzled over why John Knight – or rather 200 Irish labourers – dammed the Barle's headwater to create Pinkworthy Pond.*

Below: *Part of what is left of the Pinkworthy canal.*

One can only marvel that Knight persisted with his vision of transforming such wilderness into fields of waving corn.

Bleak though it can appear, Pinkworthy attracts pretty damsel flies such as this.

trucks up steep inclines at the Simonsbath end. The railway would have been used for transporting South Wales limestone (though curiously there was lime to be had nearby) from the coast and as his farms became more productive could have taken produce away. He might also have been thinking of his mineral rights and the possibility of exploiting them. Whatever his intentions, he failed to reach an agreement for the railway and buildings to cross another estate and the lake remains, eerie and enigmatic. A friend who decided to skinny-dip in it, emerged bright red, as befits the name! Another grand plan, to build a 'handsome residence' behind Boevey's old house, Simonsbath House, also came to nothing, and the shell was pulled down after some sixty years.

Two years after handing over to Frederic, Knight ran out of energy and retired to Rome where he died in 1850. He was kept fully informed of what was happening on Exmoor though and it is certain that he genuinely loved and intimately knew the moor in all its moods. His biggest mistake was in trying to tame it almost single-handed – with only his sons and hired hands to help him. Frederic, having been brought up on the moor could see where his father had gone wrong and set about putting things right, but he too was in for a rough ride. His father's schemes had cost dear and because he had

not colonised the moor, there was little coming in from rents. Frederic pressed ahead with the creation of tenant farms – Emmett's Grange, Driver, Duredown, Warren, Horsen, Winterhead, Pinkworthy, Tom's Hill and Larkbarrow. Frederic had also realised that his father should have created more windbreaks and instructed his agent to plant beech hedges, the first to be grown on such a huge scale. It was not plain sailing. Tenants came forward but some fled in the face of the task ahead, without signing. Others just could not hack the harsh conditions and did not last. During these tricky times, from around 1850 to 1860, Frederic, with characteristic energy, combined his duties as MP for West Worcestershire and in the City, with mining ventures and experimenting with a grass and root rotation method which would become the basis of successful large-scale sheep ranching on Exmoor. In 1856 the church of St Luke was built and blessed, and a school was built. Simonsbath was now properly the heart of a parish – the Ecclesiastical and Civil Parish of Exmoor, with 281 people living on the Knight estate and 30 children attending the school. It is still the largest parish in Somerset – with just 75 houses.

Warren Farm – one of Knight's farms though tradition has it that a house stood here much earlier – mounds nearby, and the name, indicate that this was the site of a warren, or conygar, to supply rabbits for the table.

Larkbarrow Farm was one of John Knight's model farms and only reduced to such ruination when Exmoor became a wartime training ground.

However, country-wide farming depression was to see three-quarters of a million farmers and farmworkers emigrate, and Knight needed to find a way of increasing revenues. His only option was to increase his own sheep flocks. In his biggest and boldest experiment yet, 5000 Blackface and Cheviot ewes were brought to Exmoor from the Scottish Highlands and Borders, their shepherds coming with them to settle on the moor. At last, sixty years on from his father's beginnings, the right type of farming for the moor had come about and Frederic Knight tasted success. The tenant farms were also improving, with local men who knew the terrain and Knight's methods, taking them over.

After all that had gone before – and his mining venture that also derailed – life should have have tasted sweet. But in 1879, his only son, also Frederic, died aged twenty-eight, dashing his father's dreams of handing on his legacy and breaking his heart. He was nearing seventy and had lost his stomach for experimentation and reclamation. The financial difficulties that had dogged him since his father's death were still present in the form of a hefty mortgage and he decided reluctantly that to enjoy his remaining years he must sell the whole of the Exmoor and Brendon estates. One sale fell through, it seems because he was concerned about speculators

getting their hands on the estates and eventually he sold to Lord Fortescue of Castle Hill at Filleigh, just off the moor, but retained a life interest in them, which he continued to enjoy for another eleven years. When Frederic died, followed three years later by his wife, and the mortgage was discharged, some £70,000 was left, not a huge sum in consideration of all that had been spent and his father's initial outlay. But though there are undoubtedly many stories of ordinary men and women, which have to belong to another book, it was the Knights' vision that created the community at the heart of this moor and its unique landscape of wild moorland and farms and pastureland that we see today. The house that Boevey built has seen many changes in its 325-year existence: allowed to run to ruin, licensed as an inn in 1789 and probably a smuggler's lair, hunting lodge, school and for the past thirty years the Simonsbath House Hotel.

Above: *East Pinford Stell.*

Opposite above: *Enclosure for sheep, also known as Buscombe Beeches, at Lanacombe, almost certainly dating to Frederic Knight's time – beech was planted to provide extra shelter.*

Opposite below: *Sheep stell – a form of sheep shelter introduced by the Scottish shepherds – at Three Combes Foot.*

Lone tree.

Chapter 9

&

A LIVING ON THE LAND

The enigma of Exmoor's living landscape lies in its apparent continuity and serenity, a pattern of settlement and livelihood in essence much as it was in Saxon times. Painted with the broadest brush, it is a landscape shaped by farming from before Domesday, a record of how people lived in the past in their hamlets, villages and towns, encircling the uninhabited wasteland that was the Royal Forest.

Mansley Combe.

But the devil is in the detail. Farms and villages failed; tracks that served for centuries became roads; wooden and rough cob buildings crumbled to be replaced in stone, or not; medieval buildings often were adapted and absorbed through the ages; enclosure and reclamation reshaped the scenery; old practices faded away. So much change and turmoil, hidden from show in today's tranquil scene. Inevitably, the major players and their grand gestures tend to take centre stage. Ordinary everyday folk – from farmer to fuller,

poacher to parson, miller to miner – in the teeth of climate deterioration and dramatic fluctuation, got on with eking a living from the moor, leaving little to show. In doing so they are part of a special and sparse breed, and part of the specialness of Exmoor, but we can only touch on their lives here. Their stories – mostly it has to be said of men not women – are there in patchy fashion in surviving documents and archives, translated and often traced on the ground by authors such as McDermot, S.H.Burton, Roger A. Burton, Hazel Eardley-Wilmot and Hope Bourne, to make great fireside reading. It is worth following in their footsteps to gain a feel for these medieval times.

We can catch glimpses out there, in places trapped in time. Exmoor's five major deserted settlements, at Badgworthy, Mansley Combe, Ley Hill, Grexy Combe and Sweetworthy, hold invaluable information about medieval life. They are unblurred by later additions or developments like the medieval settlements that did endure and adapt, offering archaeologists invaluable information on how the people who occupied them lived. You feel that field patterns and boundaries have much to tell but are more difficult for the ordinary walker to interpret. And if you have ever got lost in the network of tiny lanes and wondered why they are there, these too are a clue, directly reflecting the scattered nature of Exmoor's settlement.

The enduring thread that over the centuries dominated everyone's lives and livelihood, apart from those few on the coast and fertile lowlands, was sheep. Too wet and high for corn, the land had plenty of grass and rough pasture. The isolated farmsteads – still Exmoor's main settlement feature – were out in the combes and sheltered hillsides on spring-lines for water, sited where the farmer was near to his flocks, particularly in winter and lambing time. In the farmhouses and cottages of the hamlets the wool was spun, to be collected by merchants to be woven, fulled, dyed and finished in thriving towns like Dunster, whose famous Yarn Market is still at the heart of the town. In North Molton, from where thousands of sheep were taken onto the moor each year for pasturage, a stapler's mark can still be seen on the wall of Red Lion House. The initials may well be those of Thomas Parker, a wealthy wool merchant, whose family later left the village and would become the Morleys of magnificent Saltram House in South Devon.

As we have seen, hamlets often grew up around a barton, perhaps with a parish church. Commonly on Exmoor, the barton farm and parish church stand together, as at Upton near Brompton Regis, and Barton Town, Challacombe. The pattern tended to be haphazard as a barton was added to organically. Larger, more nucleated villages do occur but are less common. These might be near a ford or stream that could power a water mill, and perhaps have a forge. As fortunes fluctuated so bartons became hamlets and sometimes the reverse, as at Wilmersham Farm, now a single holding, but almost certainly once a hamlet. At East Lynch, now owned by the National Trust, roof timbers have been dated by dendrochronology to give an exact felling date of 1316. Buildings such as these reveal the materials that would have been commonly used – sometimes cob, sometimes unmortared roughly coursed stone and probably thatch as no roofing material has been found, and also how the collections of houses, shippons and barns were laid out.

Perhaps the most atmospheric deserted village is Badgworthy, home of R.D. Blackmore's infamous Doones. Though no doubt most of us are drawn by the atmosphere of the Doone mythology, Badgworthy happens to be also one of the finest pieces of undisturbed medieval landscape in the South West. Blackmore describes it:

> *But further down, on wither bank, were covered houses built of stone, square and roughly cornered, set as if the brook were meant to be the street between them. Only one room high as they were, and not placed opposite each other, but in and out as skittles are.*

Badgworthy would have been already been abandoned for some 200 years before the Doones supposedly lived (*Field Archaeology of Exmoor*) and is a remarkable record of an isolated community in the thirteenth and fourteenth centuries. The name means Baga's Farm

Dunster's famous Yarn Market.

Badgworthy Water in Doone country.

and though not mentioned in the Domesday Book, its proximity to Bronze Age barrows suggests it attracted human occupation in those times. It was given to the Knights Hospitallers in the twelfth century and described as the land of the hermits of Baga Wordia, though who they were is a mystery. By the thirteenth century a priest and chapel are recorded but by 1423 the buildings were all but deserted. In the early nineteenth century only an old man named Tucker and his granddaughter lived there and they died in a snowstorm in the winter of 1814/15, whether or not cast out into it by real-life Doones!

Blackmore also refers to a 'telling house' as a landmark where young John Ridd was supposed to be met by his father, thus pinpointing the pivotal role of sheep both in and around the Royal Forest. Telling was the shepherds' word for counting (a Norman word) the sheep as they were moved backwards and forwards from their summer pasturages so that fees could be levied. In one of the Forest books the number of telling houses is given as four; the few crumbling ruins remaining on Exmoor have caused much debate over their true locations. In the eighteenth century the highest proportion of sheep came from the south-western edge of the moor. In 1736 there were 30,000 sheep in the Forest, a quarter of them from North Molton. But they came from as far away as Landkey and Swimbridge, even Bishop's Tawton. Picturing thousands of sheep being driven some 20 miles or more to their summer grazing helps to illustrate the sheer scale of enterprise and how vital a cog they were in the livelihood of just about everyone. Even in the twenty-first century, with the wool industry gone and the whole economic value of sheep in flux if not meltdown, they still seem integral to the landscape – but how different it must have looked in those times and how different it may soon look.

Around the Forest the commons were vital to everyday life for both small-scale husbandry that provided food for the table and the rights of turbary – the digging of peat and cutting of furze and heather for fuel, lighting and roofing. The farmsteads that ringed the Forest followed a pattern of small in-fields, the 'in-bye' to which the ewes were brought for lambing, and bigger ones, further away, for spring grazing, hay and domestic crops. A common feature of Exmoor's landscape is the curving boundary enclosing a farm holding that marked the intake of land from the waste or woodland, perhaps evolving over centuries. In some places, such as Challacombe and Parracombe, can be seen evidence of strip lynchets where in-fields were worked close to the hamlet. These may well indicate on Exmoor, as elsewhere, how a mixed system of agriculture, because of a deteriorating climate, gave way to pastoralism. But there is also evidence that large areas of the commons were cultivated in field patterns that were swallowed up by later enclosure. Though quite visible in the landscape, on Winsford Common for example, and characterised by low field banks and areas of slight ridge and furrow, they are absent from historical records, posing something of a mystery.

The farmed land was separated from the commons by strong hedge-banks and each farmer had his own moor-gate for taking his flocks onto the commons and beyond into the Forest. These now are only names: Cloutsham Gate, Dunkery Gate and Blackmoor Gate to name just three – but look out for a massive hedgebank or clear division between farmland and heath. Before the Knights brought proper roads, getting around was by means of pony, oxen along well-worn tracks, and trackamucks or truckamucks – mentioned by Hoskins and Southey also – which were a crude sort of sledge fashioned from a couple of trees fastened to the horse. By the late-eighteenth and nineteenth centuries, as war brought food shortages driving agricultural reform, many field enclosures took on the larger more regimented pattern as ordered by parliamentary edict; many hamlets had been amalgamated into single farmsteads; many farmsteads were quietly deserted. Conversely it was also the heyday of the great estate which tended to reflect not Exmoor so much as their owners' dreams and aspirations, from John Knight's vision of fields of corn, to the Italianate terraces of Nettlecombe or the picturesque parkland of Glenthorne.

True owners of the moor.

But as Thomas Hardy so evocatively depicts in *Far From The Madding Crow*d, the cycle of the farming year remained the backbone of ordinary society; lambing, the drifts, hay-harvest and shearing were times when the sparse and scattered community helped each other out and when at last there was a little time to relax and enjoy revelries as a welcome respite from the tough grind of the rest of the year. Though many of the families who farmed the moor from the days of Frederic Knight and later Lord Fortescue are gone and hill-farming has hobbled through many tribulations, the sense of community endures, but only just.

When Frederic Knight brought some 5000 Cheviot flocks, along with Blackface sheep from Scotland, together with their shepherds, he began a new chapter of sheep ranching on Exmoor. The Cheviots, like the native Exmoor Horn, had plenty of history, having roamed the Cheviot Hills for some six centuries. Having adapted to such harsh country they were hardy but originally carried little meat – and very little wool. However with cross-breeding the breed was perfected to produce a third more meat and wool. Notoriously, the Cheviots replaced the thousands of people driven from their homes in the Highland Clearances but such inhumanity was not the case on Exmoor which was hardly populated before 1820. Some of the sheep came by rail as far as Williton, some by sea; others followed the old drovers' trails, like those brought by Robert Tait Little who made an epic journey from Dumfries to Duredon farm in 1868. Little was a remarkable man in many ways, better educated than most of his contemporaries and a man who kept meticulous records, as well as possessing a remarkable skill in treating wounds. But he like many of the Scottish shepherds found himself the victim of Viscount Ebrington's (Lord Fortescue's son) policy of letting as many farms as possible, which saw many of the Scottish shepherds leave the moor by the new century. The Cheviots too, after some hundred years as the mainstay of the Exmoor Estate farming economy, were gradually replaced by more suitable Scotch BlackfacexCheviot ewes, further crossbred with Blackface rams.

Through it all the native Exmoor Horn, not so much the favourite breed locally as an institution, survived and thrives. Distinctive in that both sexes are horned, it is a 'chubby-looking' sheep something akin to a horned teddy bear, best seen when the animals are in full wool. It was one of the local British breeds whose wool helped to establish the high reputation of the West Country wool industry when it depended solely on home-grown wools – a good fleece may weigh around 7lbs! The meat produced by the 'Hornie' is of the finest quality and flavour. One of the Horn's major assets is the ewe's ability to produce a top-quality half-bred ewe when crossed with the Blue Faced Leicester ram – the now famous Exmoor Mule which along with Closewool Mule is highly sought after. It is the Exmoor Mule that brings buyers to South Molton Sheep Fair, Blackmoor Gate, Yarde Down and Cutcombe each autumn. As the 1908 flock book of the Breed society, founded in 1906, puts it:

> No other breed than the pure Porlock Horn sheep *[its original name]* can live or thrive on Porlock Hill because they have to share their food with the stags on a farm 800ft high where eight months of the year are winter.

South Molton's sheep fair survives into the twenty-first century, as does the market now back in action after the foot and mouth in 2001. North Devon, Dunster and Exford Shows are also highspots for seeing top-quality specimens in hot competition with each other. Further afield, the most prestigious showcase of all, the Royal Smithfield Show, always attracts a good entry of Exmoor Horns. Truly, with all that has been flung at farming over the past few years, the farmers as well their sheep must be a remarkable breed.

Casting the eye away from sheep-dotted hillside and moorland, in the next field may well stand yet another jewel in Exmoor's crown, a herd of Red Devon – also known as Red Ruby – cattle. Like the red deer, ponies, Exmoor Horn and Closewools, they are another unique breed, amongst the most ancient of all, enduring to the present and even a squaring of the circle for farming now.

Red Devons – or Rubies.

The Pilgrim Fathers took red cattle from Devon to the New World and others were probably exported to Ireland before 1580. Now they can be seen dotted all over Exmoor and numbers are increasing but the story started some three hundred years ago on the south-western corner of the moor with the James Quartly who took the leasehold of Great Champson farm at Molland in 1703. His grandson started the serious business of improving the native breed of cattle, the Devon. By the end of the eighteenth century they were considered, according to Billingsley, writing his *General View of the County of Somerset* in 1798 for the king, the best draught oxen in the kingdom. By the second half of the 1800s the Devon breed had become second only to the Shorthorn in Britain and until the 1950s the Red Ruby was the basis of all the dual-purpose herds milked in this part of the West Country They produce good meat and rich creamy milk but had to contend with an invasion of Continental breeds, such as Belgian Blue, Limousin and Simmental, used to cross-breed with dairy cattle. Fortunately for the Red Ruby the food revolution and safety concerns of the past twenty years or so have seen a return to demand for quality, untampered-with food, beef

our grandparents would have chosen, fine textured, well marbled, the traditional dish of old England and still the natural choice for a celebration feast.

Though the basis of the farm is native breeds – Devon Closewool sheep, Exmoor Horn sheep and Exmoor ponies – the mainstay is the Red Rubies which in 1993 won the Devon Society's annual herd competition and have continued to amass prizes. Molland, meanwhile, proudly sports the letter R on its village plaque under the Alphabet of Parishes scheme across North Devon.

Farming is still well evident – one only has to go to South Molton's ancient pannier market on a Thursday, held below the Assembly Rooms with the town's crest bearing a fleece as well as mitre and crown, to think that perhaps things are alive and well. But things have changed, dramatically, even to the layman's eye over the past fifteen years or so. Change, as they say, happens and hopefully the resilience of centuries will continue to carry Exmoor through, but that is for another chapter.

The Alps or Exmoor?

Wet, wet, wet!

Exmoor's climate hardly needs further description but in fact the weather is as varied as the landscape. Generally it is influenced by the prevailing 'warm, wet westerlies', winds bringing moist air off the Atlantic and warmed by the Gulf Stream. Thus the south-western edge of the moor has the highest rainfall and snowfall and those with any sense head to the rain-shadow areas of the north-east part to retire! Gardens here are notably some four to six weeks ahead of those on the south side in spring. Annual precipitation on The Chains at 1600ft (487m) is over 2000mm compared to 80mm to the east of the moor. But such a varied area sees dramatic variations in temperature and rainfall figures within short distances. Between Dunkery and the Vale of Porlock the rainfall drops by half in as little as 2 miles.

Though winters have become milder since around 1970 – as seen by the arrival of Dartford Warblers, the early flowering of primroses and nothing like the snows of yesteryear – they can be extremely cold and wet, particularly on the higher upland areas, naturally. The Exmoor pony's special double coat evolved over thousands of years to enable it endure such conditions. The moor is certainly not immune to snow and in years of heavy falls, the deep lanes have remained cut off for long periods.

Dunkery is traditionally the local weatherglass, the saying going that 'When Dunkery's top cannot be seen, Horner will have a flooded stream'. Another reckons, 'If you can see Wales it is going to rain; if you can't it is already raining.'

Dartford Warbler.

Illustration: Sheila Wilkinson

What's in a Name?

As surnames became more fixed in medieval times they often reflected people's occupations, as can be seen on Exmoor.

Webster – a female Webber, a word for weaver no longer used, associated with the wool industry.

Tucker – Very common on Exmoor and also to do with the wool industry, a person who fulled or tucked the cloth. Derived from the word torment, because the tucker tormented the cloth.

Fuller – See above.

Walker – after weaving, the cloth was cleaned – known as fulling – originally by men trampling the cloth in troughs of water – and called walkers.

Lister, Lester, Ledstar – from lyster, another word for a dyer.

Baxter – a female baker.

Brewster – a female brewer.

Kembers, Kempsters and Carders – combed the wool ready for spinning.

And also

Spinster (though not a surname) – the archaic name for an unmarried woman derives from the days when the females in their cottages did the spinning.

Chapter 10

OF MINES AND MEN

Strangers often accost residents in North Molton, on the edge of the moor, designated by its brown sign as 'Historic Mining Village', to ask where they can see the mines. The usual answer has to be that the closest they are likely to get is one of the village's two pubs, the Miners Arms. Like the rest of Exmoor's long and chequered history of mining, dating at least to Roman and perhaps to Iron Age times, the evidence is fading into the landscape, even though the last iron mines were worked into the last century to the end of the First World War.

Most minerals found beneath the surface and outcropping on Exmoor are associated with the folded Devonian slates and sandstones, shot into the existing rocks during the time of continental collision and volcanic activity some 300 million years ago. Iron and copper were the main ones to reach Exmoor, along with smaller amounts of zinc, silver-lead, manganese, antimony – and gold, which would provoke the inevitable folly and greed of men. The rest of the story is a curious melting pot of failure, boom and bust, epic struggle and endurance, seen now only as a handful of relics in the landscape.

Iron ore is present around North Molton and a vein known as Roman Lode seems to run across Exmoor from Simonsbath to the Brendon Hills where the lodes of ore are at their richest. Workings at Cornham Ford could be Roman but may date from the sixteenth century. The ores around North Molton are the only ones with high enough copper ore worth exploiting, the Bampfylde mine and Britannia mine also yielding gold. Iron has been mined in the area on and off for centuries, the major boom time being in the latter part of the nineteenth century. It is reckoned that at one time the village had more than a dozen drinking establishments to satisfy the miners' thirst. On pay nights some of them stayed open all night and were full to the following morning. The work-hard, play-hard miners were also to be found adding a lusty presence to local revelries such as the North Molton Great Fair and May Fair which are now lost, like the mines.

Silver-lead ore outcrops around Combe Martin and workings are recorded from the thirteenth century when Edward I's daughter Eleanor received a dowry of 270lb of Combe Martin silver. In the reign of Elizabeth I a new and lucrative silver lode was worked, and in the nineteenth century several brooches of Combe Martin silver were bought by Queen Victoria. The name Eisen, the German word for iron was given to a hill near Winsford by German miners who were brought over to this country in Elizabeth's time, their mining technology being far in advance of ours. At that time, amazingly, the

Knapp Down silver mine at Combe Martin.

copper mines at Molland were the most productive in the world though perhaps the heyday of the industry was the late nineteenth century when Exmoor mines supplied ore to the burgeoning iron and steel industry of South-Wales.

At the time of writing there is also excitement over recent findings that point to Roman iron working being on a much larger scale than had been thought – which may yet mean a rewriting of previous thinking on Roman Exmoor. Excavation of a massive Roman iron production site at Sherracombe revealed the enormous scale of iron production on the site with solid blocks of iron slag weighing up to 20kg being found.

The principal nineteenth-century iron mining developments took place on the Brendons, where the ore is siderite (iron carbonate), and lasted for nearly fifty years. Its potential was discovered around the 1840s and the Brendon Hills Mining Co. was formed in 1852 and began work at Ralegh's Cross. The Brendons were a good source of the non-phosphatic iron ore required for the new Bessemer steel-making process. To make it viable a new railway, the West Somerset Mineral Railway, had to be built, bringing the tranquillity of the Valley of Flowers, as the Roadwater valley was known, to an end, while Watchet harbour was developed as the outlet for the ore to the furnaces of South Wales. At its height in 1877 output hit nearly 47,000 tons but within five years competition from Spanish ores and a new process that could use any ore, changed everything. In 1883 the mines at Brendon Hill and Gupworthy were closed with just six months' notice.

The most powerful steam engines were at the large Ralegh's Cross Mine. The buildings were demolished in 1907 and a few mounds in a field are all that is to be seen now. Burrow Farm Mine, in contrast, has the only surviving engine house, reminiscent of those found in Cornwall and in fact partly built by Cornish miners. Built in 1880, it was, ironically, only in operation for three years. The Brendon mineral line connected the iron mines along the ridge of the

Ruins of Burrow Farm Mine engine house.

Brendon Hills and in turn connected to a line to Watchet via a steep incline which ran from Ralegh's Cross. Laden trucks descended the incline by gravity and empty trucks were winched back up by a steam engine set below the track at the top. It was said that the cost of constructing the incline would equal the cost of covering its surface with gold sovereigns but when it was sold in 1924 it raised just £15. About half of the trackbed of the lower section is now either a public footpath or highway, and both it and the engine house are now owned by the National Park Authority.

At the heart of Exmoor the Knights were convinced that their own land must hold similar potential. It was to be a long-drawn out and costly saga of failure and disappointment – for which Exmoor can only be grateful. Had they been successful, who knows what scars the landscape might now bear.

Near Simonsbath, about a mile along the River Barle, can be seen the remains of Wheal Eliza, the main focus of their dreams of striking it rich. Before long John had retired to Rome and Frederic granted the lease to a local syndicate, described as a 'company of adventurers', which worked Eliza for copper for nearly ten years from 1846–55 – to little avail. A shaft, adit, waste dumps and ruined miners' cottages survive, while across the Barle a leat leads to the site of a pumping wheel. When copper comparable to the best that the Bampfylde mine at Heasley Mill could produce was found, the project looked set fair. It must have been difficult to attract workers to such a wild and isolated spot, though they are there on the 1851 Census; mine captains came and went, and in 1848 heavy rains and flooding halted work several times. At last, according to William Thornton, the first curate of the Parish of Exmoor and friend of the Knights, it seemed that a rich vein had been encountered in May 1849. Efforts were redoubled and more money ploughed in, but year upon year saw a familiar pattern; flooding, drought, small but promising finds that soon petered out, miners quitting and ultimately shareholders' revolt. Over £10,000 and years of sweated labour resulting in a 300ft shaft with crosscuts east and west,

Wheal Eliza, with stumps of cottages behind.   D. Coxon

Gravestone of the ill-fated Anna Maria Burgess.

produced nothing more than a few tons of decent ore. Between 1856–59 it reopened, to be worked for iron by Schneider & Hannay, but once more the quantities found made it unviable.

Notoriously, Wheal Eliza acquired a bleak cachet as the spot chosen by a man named Burgess to conceal the body of his young daughter Anna Maria whom he had murdered. The stories of how she met her end have differed wildly but the remains of the little girl of six, whose only 'crime' was to have been a nuisance to her feckless father, were found in the shaft after a long and arduous operation to drain the flooded mine. Burgess by this time had been traced to South Wales and brought back to Dulverton Gaol, then to Taunton to stand trial. Having been found guilty and sentenced to death he confessed his guilt, explaining that the child was in his way and everyone else's and he had thought she would be 'better off out of it'. He was hanged at Taunton in front of a large crowd, which included two of his other, older, children, who it seems were not surprised to hear of his appalling crime. Wheal Eliza was never worked again.

Knight remained convinced that there were large reserves of ore beneath his land and around 1856 three companies – Schneider & Hannay, the Plymouth Iron Co. and Dowlais Iron Works – were at work on Knight's land at various sites including Picked Stones, Blue Gate, Cornham Ford, Burcombe and Honeymead. They too must have been confident, as Schneider & Hannay agreed to pay £7000 towards the railway that was badly needed to get the ore away efficiently, while Dowlais agreed to supply the rails and took on a forty-two year lease. As it would transpire, events followed a similar pattern as at Wheal Eliza, with good finds petering to nothing and much abortive and costly exploration. Schneider & Hannay cut their losses and quit though it cost them £10,000 for breaking their contract; the Plymouth Co. faded away and eventually, by around 1860, Dowlais too gave up the struggle. Knight had at last got the agreement he needed to take his railway across Porlock Common but it was too late. Although the rails were never put down, the course was prepared and much of the 9-mile route can be traced, for example near Larkbarrow Corner. Dowlais preferred to cut their losses by paying him £7000: another hugely costly venture. It was the end of mining of iron ore during Knight's time though prospecting went on, one report even stating that a company of adventurers proposed to work Knight's properties on a grand scale. Nothing came of it.

Interest was revived around the turn of the century but it was nearly a decade later before any work got underway. The Picked

All that remains of Wheal Eliza, though still fenced off for safety, seen mid-right.

Stones site, one of those investigated by the Plymouth Iron Co. in the late 1850s, was one of the sites now worked by the Exmoor Mining Syndicate from around 1910 and proved the most productive. A tramway was built to the nearest road so that ore could be carried to Dulverton station but the many and various schemes for railways and aerial walkways totted up to prohibitive costs, and carrying ore off the moor by traction engine would prove ruinous both for the roads and any profit from the ore. In 1912 and 1913 particularly atrocious weather created appalling conditions for the miners, and affected operations; it seems the curse on Exmoor's potential mineral wealth would never be beaten. Ultimately, the problem of transport was the last straw and by the outbreak of the Great War the mines were quiet again. Further efforts and grandiose schemes to restart them failed despite interest from the Ministry of Munitions.

It is difficult to hit the right balance in relating something of Exmoor's mining history: in evaluating its importance as a 'living from the land' and to our 'discovery' of Exmoor, when it has all but disappeared back into the landscape. It has been computed that millions of tons of iron ore lie beneath the now tranquil surface and that this was known and exploited by our ancient ancestors, perhaps as far back as the Iron Age. Archaeological work yields new understanding, and exploration has continued around North Molton and Combe Martin areas, while uranium has been found near Simonsbath. Throughout the ages, miners have come from outside – Cornwall, Germany and other places – but they had to be fed and watered and there must have been some knock-on benefit deriving from these episodes. Any new attempts at mining would certainly now be resisted by the National Park Authority, so it seems certain that the chapter is closed for ever. Then again …

Chapter 11

MARITIME EXMOOR

The coast, where the moor plunges sometimes dizzyingly into the sea, is in many ways like another country, yet impossible to divorce from its moorland hinterland and the Royal Forest. Moorland becomes maritime in such short order that the contrasts are the more stunning. The coast is as spectacular as the moorland is magnificent, with cliffs the highest in England, and in 1991 it was designated a Heritage Coast. Where the heathland meets the sea, be you on Great Hangman, Woody Bay or perhaps Bossington Hill, is to experience Exmoor with all the senses: drinking in clear air scented with gorse and the tang of sea breezes, the vibrant colours, and hearing the calls of seabirds, raven and buzzard. In the woodlands of sessile oak, yew and rare whitebeams, reaching down almost onto the beach, woodland birds such as woodpeckers and jays mingle with seabirds like fulmars and oystercatchers.

Countisbury Foreland, looking down on Sillery Sands.

The Bristol Channel, once known so much more romantically as the Severn Sea, is remarkable for a 40ft rise and fall of the tides, second only in the world to that of the Bay of Fundy in Canada. Headlands that face west are battered by Atlantic gales and have vertical cliff faces, as on Great Hangman reaching 800ft (250m) but the characteristic rounded hog's-back shape echoes the shape of the Exmoor hills as they slope more gently towards the sea.

You can almost picture, as topographer Page did in 1890, a sea 'covered with shipping', which in three little words conjures up an evocative picture of bygone times and a way of life very different from that of the Royal Forest, the inner moor. The coastal settlements, Lynmouth, Combe Martin and Porlock Weir all developed initially as fishing harbours and ports for trade in the Bristol Channel and elsewhere. Thatched fishermen's cottages and old lime-kilns echo this

Mars Hill and harbour, Lynmouth, a scene little changed over centuries.

past. Smuggling was for many a way of life – few saw anything much wrong with giving HM Customs & Excise a run for their money.

Sloops and ketches plied back and forth bringing slates from Cornwall, supplies from Bristol, taking pit-props from the coastal woods to South Wales, returning with coal and limestone. Times were slow to change, even as tourism slowly crept in, because until late in the nineteenth century there was still no turnpike or railway along Exmoor's unforgiving coastline. As with the harshness of moorland life, the coast was a hard mistress; the frequency of shipwrecks saw the rescue service grow in importance, with many incidences of heroism, like that of the amazing overland launch of the *Louisa*.

On the tempestuous night of 12 January 1899, a full-rigged iron ship, the *Forrest Hall*, was in trouble in huge seas in Porlock Bay and the call went out to launch the Lynmouth lifeboat, the *Louisa*. It soon proved impossible in the teeth of such a storm, whereupon coxswain and crew set out to haul the boat 15 miles overland. Into the darkness went the crew, a dozen or so carthorses and much of the population who had come out to help in the gruelling task of lugging the 3½ ton boat up Countisbury Hill onto the moorland ridge road. Here part of the road was too narrow for the carriage so the boat was taken off and hauled on skids while the carriage was taken separately over open ground. Even so part of the wall along the road had to be dismantled, yet the journey was completed in about thirteen hours and before first light the next day the crew went alongside the *Forrest Hall*. They helped a tug tow the crippled ship to Barry so it was five that afternoon when the exhausted crew were finally done, or more likely done in. But they had achieved a successful rescue and each of the crew received a silver watch as a memento. The tale was faithfully re-enacted a century later on 12 January 1999 and graphically illustrated the enormousness of their achievement.

In the same way that the tidal range results from the funnelling effect of the Channel, so it provides in the Vale of Porlock a warm, moist micro-climate making it a little land of plenty. One of the most fertile areas in the Park, it is still fêted for the finest malting barley. Combe Martin in the sheltered Umber Valley became the 'garden of Exmoor', renowned for market gardening. In 1326 William Martin, last of the family the village is named for, is recorded as growing fruit. The village boasted that its strawberries were at least ten days earlier than anywhere else in the country and in its market gardening heyday, school would close so that pupils could join the whole village out picking in the fields – they might have preferred lessons to the back-breaking job of picking strawbs!

Combe Martin – garden of Exmoor.

On the south side of the valley can be seen evidence of medieval strip fields with high hedges which were later enclosed into bigger plots. Shute Lane, running along a ridge above these strips is probably so named because a 'shute' was the strip of land on which the plough teams on open fields were turned. A major crop from Tudor times was hemp which thrived in fertile soil and warm, sheltered fields. Reputedly the best in the country, it was used for rope and cord making and shoemaker's thread. Market gardening took over in the

The verdant Vale of Porlock, renowned for its barley.

early nineteenth century, supplying to the infant tourist trade of Ilfracombe which was a genteel resort until the First World War, with a clientele able to afford luxury delicacies. With high transport costs and competition from larger-scale players, few market gardeners are left but a handful plough on, growing some fruit and veg, and strawberries and cut flowers that can still be seen temptingly displayed at Barnstaple's Pannier Market. Another local speciality, though a matter of taste, still on offer nearby on Butcher's Row and all around Exmoor, is laver, a type of edible seaweed, which Combe Martin women would collect from the shoreline. The path on the Rawns between Great and Little Hangman, was treacherous and there were many fatal accidents from slipping or drowning.

St Beuno's churchyard where lie the Red family.

In the heavily wooded coastal stretch that extends west from Porlock Weir to Glenthorne, Culbone Woods were and still are almost another country. Their isolated position seems always to have attracted outcasts, like the leper colony who are reputed to have made a living from charcoal burning. They were not allowed to cross over to the Porlock side of Culbone Water and the leper-squint window in the north side of the nave of the tiny church of St Beuno – acclaimed as the smallest complete parish church in England – allowed them to join in worship from outside in the churchyard. Later burners, some of them former French prisoners of war and their descendants, were no longer restricted like the lepers and traded their charcoal at Porlock Weir. Bark-stripping was also carried on to supply the leather tanning industry.

In St Beuno's churchyard lie members of the Red and Redd families, their name according to some derived from the staining of their bodies in the tanning business. Bark was exported from Lynmouth to Wales and from Porlock to Cornwall, though some was used for 'barking' the fishermen's ropes and sails, whereby they were steeped in an infusion of oak-parings to proof them against rot.

The oak was also felled to supply timbers for shipbuilding, while ash was coppiced for building and farm implements, hazel was cut for hurdles and thatching spars, and willow or withy for weaving into baskets and such like. In Culbone Woods, the remains of the charcoal burners' huts, their pits and the saw-pits remained visible for a long time.

Another commodity that gave work to men of the coast and moor, the importance of which is still visible in the landscape, was lime, used since Roman times for mortar and to improve soil; 48 limekilns in various stages of ruination, still exist on Exmoor. The more permanent structures date to the eighteenth century onwards as demand was driven by agricultural improvement. Ten of them lie along the coast, either in harbours, such as Porlock Weir or Lynmouth, or on the shingle beaches where boats could pull up and offload their cargoes, as at Bossington beach, Glenthorne and Embelle Woods. The example on Bossington beach is unusual in being freestanding as most were built into an embankment or cliff. Much of the limestone came from South Wales and the Exmoor 'lime-captains' who sailed the ketches had to know the coast as surely as smugglers so that they could run their cargo ashore for kilns such as Bossington and Heddon's Mouth.

Limestone quarrying was another living to be found on the coast with three main quarries and many smaller ones on Exmoor, the Brendons and the Quantocks.

Left: *Limekiln at Heddon's Mouth.*

Below: *Restored limekiln at Woody Bay.*

Left: *Limekiln at Combe Martin.*

Roofing slates from Treborough quarry were used for Dunster Castle in 1425, though apparently the cost of transporting them was double the coast of the slates themselves. More intensive working, producing roofing slates, chimney tops, hearth and shelving stones, steps, staddle stones, sills, headstones and more, went on from the late eighteenth century, through to the late 1930s when the quarry was finally closed. Since abandonment, the main quarry has been infilled but the dressing floors, wheelpit, tunnel and the extensive tips survive in woodland.

Red herrings and Romantics

Fishing provided a living back to Mesolithic times and continued down through the centuries. By the end of the fifteenth century large vessels fished hundreds of miles off the Exmoor coast, out into the Atlantic. Early in the seventeenth century the arrival of large shoals of herring in the Bristol Channel brought relative prosperity shared in by the people of the North Devon and West Somerset coast for two hundred years. Porlock Weir and Lynmouth had red herring houses – so called because of the colour of the fish when smoked. The industry declined as catches fell, and the red herring huts, always vulnerable to storm damage, disappeared from the landscape too. Closer to home, the shingle nature of much of the foreshore and the unusual tidal range, gave rise to another method of 'harvesting' dating back to medieval times. Fish weirs – from which Porlock Weir takes its name, rather than the more usual meaning – in the Severn estuary have been dated by dendrochronology and radiocarbon dating of some wooden structures point to a date as early as the ninth century. Built of large beach cobbles shaped in a V with the point facing seawards, they worked by means of nets fixed at the seaward end, catching the fish as the tide ebbed. Whitebait were caught this way at Lynmouth into the twentieth century. Altogether 15 survive on Exmoor's coast: at Lynmouth one became the town's swimming pool. Several survive at Porlock Weir, visible at very very low tide. Oysters were also an important part of the fishing economy.

Lone reminder of Porlock Weir's fishing heyday.

As the herring deserted, as luck would have it, came a new 'catch' – tourists – sparked around the turn of the nineteenth century, by the new Romantics' admiration of the Exmoor coast's beautiful scenery and the fashion for sea-bathing, and later by those seeking Blackmore's Doone Country. Though Madame d'Arblay (the former Fanny Burney) in 1817 bemoaned the popularity of Ilfracombe, 'the Multitude has warped what the Individual has enjoyed,' she was perhaps being a tad sniffy. With the lack of decent roads, early travellers such as the Wordsworths and Coleridge had to be intrepid and thought nothing of tramping 30 miles to explore the coast. Page wrote in 1890 that along the coast road there was very little traffic:

> … except a carriage or two of folks on pleasure bent, or the gaily painted coaches … thickly packed with tourists, who are eager to know which is the Doone Valley, and whether they can see Oare Church.

In any case Exmoor 'proper', with its rugged coast and limited access to the shore had only two coastal settlements that fitted the bill, Lynmouth and Porlock. But, as the herring shoals deserted and fishing declined, the trade that came as Lynmouth became a resort, and Lynton grew with it must have been welcome to locals. It was all a very genteel and pleasantly efficient affair by all accounts. In summer a steamer service ran twice a week from Bideford to Bristol

Peaceful Porlock Weir, at least when not beset by storms.

and back, anchoring off Lynmouth where smaller boats ferried passengers ashore. There was a network of 'horse-bus' routes connecting with Barnstaple, Tiverton, Plymouth, Bridgwater, Taunton and even London. In terrain where roads were at a premium, it was said that London-bound passengers who changed at Minehead for Taunton, might have endured a bumpy ride but never failed to connect with the express train from Exeter to the capital – enough to make a twenty-first century traveller weep! At National Trust owned Arlington Court, a newly opened collection of coaches gives a good picture of those early days. But Exmoor really got on the map in 1898 when the narrow-gauge railway from Barnstaple was opened, reaching Lynton by way of Blackmoor Gate and Woody Bay. In fact Lynmouth and Lynton, since 1890, already boasted their own feat of Victorian engineering in the remarkable water-powered cliff railway, designed by Lynmouth builder and engineer Bob Jones, who also built the Foreland lighthouse. The first of its kind, the railway is still going strong as a visitor attraction today.

Above: *Lynton's Victorian cliff railway with old limekiln below.*

Left: *Lynton and Lynmouth from The Cleaves.*

Sunset at the Valley of Rocks.

Chapter 12

&

SAINTS AND SINNERS

Over much of the Exmoor landscape, the relatively few buildings blend harmoniously into the picture, seeming to have evolved with the landscape, as indeed many have. From castle to cot, and from holy place to hostelry, Exmoor has a wealth of fascinating buildings though so sparsely populated over the centuries and still home to only about 11,000 people.

With the transience of Saxon structures, they effectively date from the Norman Conquest when churches, castles and monasteries became a feature of the landscape. Existing farmsteads and settlements were absorbed into later buildings or rebuilt. Castles were a Norman import and Exmoor has only three, Dunster being the jewel in the crown, with its fairy-tale looks and history of having remained for 900 years in the hands of just two families, the de Mohuns and the Luttrells.

Dunster Castle.

Legend has it that there was a Celtic fortress in the area where St Carantoc exhibited the 'fierce and terrible' dragon that he had tamed on the orders of Prince Arthur. Later Aluric, a Saxon, is said to have fortified the present castle site. The Norman structure was built by William de Mohun, one of the Conqueror's chief supporters, before 1086. But of what we see now, all that is left of the Normans and major additions of the thirteenth and fourteenth centuries are a tower, gateway, gatehouse and curtain wall.

The de Mohuns held the Honour of Dunster until 1376 when the reversion was sold to the Luttrells who then held the estate for exactly 600 years. Their name is still prominent in the town. Perched commandingly atop a steep conical hill high above the River Avill, its original motte and bailey are now lost under later building and landscaping. The castle was twice besieged during the Civil War, once for each side! It was first held for Parliament but in 1643 the Luttrells changed sides and this siege lasted for six months. With the king's cause already lost, starvation at last forced the garrison to surrender, but they were allowed to march out with honour. Cromwell duly ordered the castle to be slighted, a partial demolition that included the razing of the Norman keep but was not as fervent as it might have been.

In Victorian times, much rebuilding was done by the Luttrells, giving the castle the appearance we see now. Both the interior and gardens are worth visiting, the latter featuring a lovely mix of native and exotic species. Grisly evidence of the castle's less gentrified days came to light in 1869 when the skeleton of a 7ft (2m) man was found in one tower of the gatehouse that was used as a dungeon. It seems that he had been manacled to a wall by his neck, hands and feet and left to die. Conygar Tower, a landmark overlooking the town and named for the hill it stands on, was also built by the Luttrells and is purely a folly. In 1976 Lieutenant-Colonel Sir Walter Luttrell gave the castle with the grounds and gardens, including the eighteenth-century working water-mill, to the National Trust.

Much less is known of the other two Exmoor castles, Holwell and Bury Castle. Holwell, commanding a steep combe running to Heddon's Mouth, near Parracombe, probably dates to the late eleventh century and is also of motte and bailey design, more visibly so as it seems to have been in use only a short time. Bury Castle, close to the town of Dulverton, and now just a mound in the landscape, took advantage of an ideal site by reusing a previous Iron Age enclosure, though available evidence suggests that it too was used only a short time. By the late eighteenth century it was part of the Pixton Park Estate, owned by the Earl of Carnarvon who laid out drives that appear to incorporate the 'castle' as a feature.

With monasteries established in Britain from around AD500, often on suitably difficult land conducive to the hermit ethic – marsh or

Holwell Castle, near Parracombe – a perfect motte and bailey.

rock – it is curious that lonely Exmoor saw only two such houses established, Dunster being the major one, and Barlynch, near Dulverton the other, with Cleeve Abbey just off the moor's fringes.

Dunster Priory was established by about 1170, alongside the church of St George, both under the auspices of the Benedictine Bath Abbey. As the town's prosperity grew the church was added to and improved, its great bell tower being completed by the mid-1400s, and records refer to 'sumptious buildings' of the monastic buildings priory. The glorious carved rood screen of the church owes its strange position, part way down the nave, to a dispute between the monks and the townsfolk, a practical measure allowing the monks to use the east end while the town worshipped in the west end. Some of the monastic church survives as part of the west and north walls of the church but other than this the Priory has almost disappeared or been incorporated into other buildings save for its Dovecote, with 800 nesting boxes and clever circulating ladder. It is worth escaping the madding holiday crowd by walking around the back of Dunster through Priory Green to see the few remains of the Priory, the beautiful cloister garden where you can imagine monks going about their business and devotions, the Tithe Barn and the Dovecote.

St George's church, Dunster.

The priory of St Nicholas, Barlynch, was founded at the time of Henry II and was a small house of Augustinian canons. After the Dissolution the site was granted to Sir John Wallop whose naval campaigns were so robust as to have been the origin of 'wallop' in the modern sense. However, his interest in Barlynch was less so and it was never again anything grander than a farm, to the present day. It is thought that the ill-fitting east window and colonnade at Huish Champflower church may have come from Barlynch. The ruins of 800-year-old Cleeve Abbey, just off the National Park boundary, conversely offer the most complete monastic house in Somerset, with some of the finest extant cloister buildings in England. Dedicated in 1198 and named Vallis Florida – Vale of Flowers – it was a Cistercian order of monks who, whilst living a spartan existence of sleeping on bare boards and eating one meal a day, established Cleeve at the heart of the surrounding community. In 1536 the last monk was turned out at the behest of Henry VIII. Today, cared for by English Heritage, its beautiful buildings, carvings and wall paintings impress yet it is the feeling of tranquillity and peace of the site that many visitors take away with them.

Exmoor people must have been God-fearing folk in following centuries, if the wealth of churches and chapels, as varied and fascinating as the landscape itself, is anything to go by. They date mostly to about the twelfth century, after which many were altered, some acquiring a grander Perpendicular style, in prosperous times – but not all, thankfully. Whilst St George's at Dunster is the grandest, thanks to medieval wealth, Exmoor also claims some of the smallest, least spoilt and most delightful churches: St Beuno at Culbone, smallest parish church in England; Stoke Pero, which vies with Simonsbath as the highest on Exmoor; Oare church latterly of *Lorna Doone* fame; Molland and Parracombe which escaped Victorian 'improvement'; Hawkridge with its Norman door and font.

When dissatisfaction with the Church grew, for once Exmoor's isolation was no barrier to new ideas. Bearing this in mind, along with the sparseness of Exmoor's human habitation, it is remarkable that almost every hamlet also boasts a Dissenting chapel, along with some that stand alone in the countryside and others now private dwellings. John and Charles Wesley, sons of a country rector who had 19 children, around the 1730s hit the pulse of the times with their ideas seeking a return to true Christian values that would become known as Methodist. Their brother Samuel had become headmaster at Blundell's School at Tiverton, which celebrated its quatercentenary in 2004, so that as well as addressing huge crowds in northern towns and London's Blackheath, they ventured west.

They gained a following in Bristol and among Cornish tinners and certainly both preached at North Molton where there was a congregation by 1745; John Wesley preached there at least three times and at Simonsbath. Meetings would be held in cottages and farmhouses but from the middle of the century chapels were built across the the moor, often in the teeth of great hostility from squires, clergy and others who rejected such ideas. Not all were Wesleyan Methodist; as many belonged to the Bible Christians whose message appealed to the poorest working classes, farm labourers, miners and the like. Within a common humble and simple style there are interesting departures: Watchet was modelled on a Greek temple, no less, whilst Beulah on its isolated road junction in the Brendon Hills, could have been beamed in from Cornwall. The latter, built in 1861, was Bible Christian and one of three chapels at Brendon Hill serving the mining community established by the Brendon Hills Iron Ore Co. which in the 1870s was some 250 people strong. The company village was strongly teetotal, the Brendon Hill & Gupworthy Temperance Society holding sway. Now Beulah Chapel, where a weekly service is held, and a few overgrown ruins are all that remains of that once thriving community.

Whilst North Molton founded the first Wesleyan chapel in North Devon, some eighty years after John Wesley's last visit, temperance must have had a run for its money as there were also numerous alehouses where the miners could quench their thirst – 14 being

Above: *St Dubricius, Porlock, with its distinctive truncated spire.*

Right, above: *Stoke Pero church.*

Right: *Oare church.*

the popular boast. Up on the moor, standing in splendid isolation at Sandyway, the Sportsman's Inn is another lone survivor of several remote inns that saw their heyday providing some respite from the lonely and gruelling existence of moormen and miners. At Mole's Chamber an inscribed stone, the Sloley Stone, a boundary stone erected in 1742, still stands somewhat forlornly, unlike the Acland Arms that stood nearby. Nowadays all is almost spookily quiet here so again robust imagination is needed to picture a much more raucous scene. When it was first licensed around 1825 it stood at a crossroads of well-worn routes across the moor, serving the packhorse drivers and sheep and cattle drovers and being so well-placed out of reach of the law, reputedly also saw much of the illicit goods smuggled in along the North Devon coast pass through. Later the miners boosted its trade but when they left, trade declined and now only a few stones and ghosts remain. On the Simonsbath–Exford Road the Gallon House was supposedly so called because nothing less than a gallon of ale was served. Needless to say, brawls, some fatal, were common and the Gallon House later became the unlicensed Red Deer farmhouse.

Sloley Stone, a hore or boundary stone which stands at the entrance to Mole's Chamber where also stood the bleak and lonely Acland Arms.

picture-book air of tranquillity belies constant change.

Typically, cottages followed a plain and simple design and, because building stone on Exmoor is poor and cannot be cut neatly, were usually built of rubble or cob – a mixture of mud, straw, dung and horse hair. We see the result in the pretty rounded shape of corners, chimneys and pillars. More important buildings might feature small amounts of imported ashlar (dressed stone), for instance on the quoins of windows or over doorways, replaced in Victorian times by brick. Most would be limewashed to protect the porous local red sandstone from the elements – the traditional pink colour wash is said to have been made by adding pig's blood to the mix. Some had slates, from local quarries such as Treborough, hung on exposed walls. Slate was used for some roofs especially in exposed parts of the moor where the long wheat straw needed for traditional thatch could not be grown. Tall chimneys are also a local feature, often placed on the front of the cottage and frequently with a bread oven built into the back of the large open fireplace inside, the curved shape still evident on many outer walls.

Thus buildings rose and fell, from humble cot to great estate; the landscape is surprisingly littered with abandoned buildings and for every crumbling pile that tells a tale, there must be another whose story is lost. So it is in the buildings that we see today. They chart Exmoor's evolving history through their fabric and style and how they have been altered and adapted, yet their settled, often

The most typical farmhouse style seen on the moor today is the courtyard farm, often medieval or earlier in origin but with many changes. Some of them were originally hamlets that shrank to one holding. Some, such as Horsen and Winterhead that were model farms created by the Knights in the former Royal Forest, amazingly survive despite their inhospitable locations. Just as the quadrangle

Cloutsham Farm.

Haddeo but little else remains to give an idea of its glory days. Glenthorne, surrounded by some of the grandest scenery in England but set almost impossibly on the coast below the Old Burrow Roman fortlet, was a rambling manor built in the nineteenth-century by a Mr Halliday, who had relinquished Holy Orders when he came into property. One description stated how getting to it involved several hairpin bends to the house 'lying in a sort of composed lunacy' at the bottom. Though the epitome of the Romantic movement and widely regarded as a 'rich man's folly' it was for a time the centre of a vibrant agricultural estate.

of the courtyard farm offered shelter, so linhays, often built into a south-facing hillside and with enclosed haylofts above and shelter for cattle below, were designed to combat the elements. Typical rounded supporting pillars suited the rough, uncut stone, as in the cottages. In complete contrast when nineteenth-century guidebooks compared the Exmoor area to Switzerland, hotels and guesthouses, and even Cloutsham Farm, with carved gable ends and balconies were the result.

Several estates and parks flourished in the late medieval period, some through to a nineteenth-century heyday. By definition they were worlds apart from and yet had huge impact on the everyday life of moor, leaving their mark in such disparate ways as the beautiful village of Selworthy, the legacy of red deer, beech trees, Elizabethan Combe Sydenham and its deer park, Italianate gardens at Ashley Combe, Dunster Castle, Nettlecombe Court now a field studies centre, and the Carnarvon Arms at Dulverton, which seemed rooted in the Exmoor landscape until recently. Some have almost faded back into the landscape. At Ashley Combe built in the 1830s overlooking Porlock Bay, all that is left of grand Italianate terraced gardens, are overgrown ruins, the house having been demolished in the 1960s, and some distinctive estate buildings, in the style of Voysey, along the coast. At Pixton Park in the eighteenth century great landscaping schemes were undertaken and Lady Harriet's Drive can be followed for several kilometres in the valley of the River

Holnicote is a completely different story and one that is very much ongoing, now under the auspices of the National Trust. In the Acland family for more than 200 years, it was considered to be their favourite estate and known as the 'happy valley'. The estate and their concern for local people resulted in the provision of homes, as in the model village of Selworthy, schools and reading rooms, as at Allerford, and a whole range of other work – masons, carpenters, thatchers, farriers and the like. The National Trust's management

Selworthy and its bright white church.

of the estate extends far beyond overseeing farms and forestry. Training in skills from building techniques and nature conservation to archaeology and interpretation is ongoing. Care of the 60 or so thatched roofs has led to research projects and sometimes surprising results. When a trial plot of the traditional wheat used for combed wheat reed was planted, it did well despite even wetter weather than usual; traditional hazel spars are cut in coppice woodland and thatching apprenticeships have been set up.

Glenthorne, where Mr Halliday built his house in its position of 'composed lunacy'.

Chapter 13

DOONERY AND ALL THAT

Child if they ask thee who killed thee,
Say it was the Doones of Badgworthy

R.D. Blackmore

It would be almost impossible to write about Exmoor without mentioning *Lorna Doone*, the book that so perfectly distilled the moor's essence into classic melodrama. Even the Ordnance Survey map now shows the area around Badgworthy (pronounced Badgery) Water as Doone Country, and countless visitors to Exmoor have come to see and feel its atmosphere for themselves.

It nearly didn't happen. *Lorna Doone*, a 'Romance of Exmoor' by R.D. Blackmore, was published in 1869 in three volumes, having already been rejected by other publishers, and only 500 copies were printed. For two years it seemed doomed to follow his previous failures, until two things changed the fortunes of Blackmore – and Exmoor – for ever. First was a bold decision by a junior partner of the publishers to publish in one volume at six shillings. The second, though versions differ, was the marriage of Queen Victoria's daughter Princess Louise to the Marquis of Lorne, whose family history was erroneously linked by a journalist to that of the fictional Lorna.

It did the trick; Blackmore was told that *Lorna Doone* was 'going to have a run' that rapidly became a gallop. Several editions later a printing of 100,000 copies sold out within a week. The romantic heroine's name became that of many a baby girl, and as Dorset had

Badgworthy Water.

become irrevocably linked with Thomas Hardy, so too did Exmoor and Blackmore for legions of literary pilgrims.

From Exmoor's point of view, fascination and argument have raged ever since over the basis and truth of Blackmore's Doones and their evil doings. Did they ever exist on Exmoor and if so what were their origins? Was there even a Doone folklore here at all, before Blackmore wrote his novel? Blackmore's own reticence was no help. He once wrote: 'Nothing will induce me to go into the genesis of Lorna Doone ... of which I have heard enough.'

He did, though, tell a correspondent that it was helping with a story that appeared in 1863, called 'The Doones of Exmoor' for *The Leisure Hour* magazine, that 'gave him the clue for the weaving of the romance, and caused him to study the details on the spot.' And in a footnote to Chapter V in which John Ridd relates how the Doones destroyed a rich man's house near Minehead, he states that 'this vile deed was done beyond all doubt.'

It seems likely that he must already have heard something of the stories from his boyhood. His grandfather had held the livings of Oare and Combe Martin, an uncle was at Charles rectory, on the edge of the moor, and he was a pupil at Blundell's School in Tiverton, attended for a while by his fictional narrator John Ridd, who is certainly to some extent autobiographical. A few years before writing the book, he revisited many of his childhood haunts, talking to locals and delving into old records.

It was probably Blackmore's masterstroke to cut through the morass of wildly differing stories abroad on Exmoor to create his blood-thirsty brigands, holed up in the old Badgworthy cots in around 1620, raiding, robbing and murdering for a living until being driven out in about 1699.

The truth could lie just about anywhere. Some tales have it that the Doones turned fugitive after joining the ill-starred Duke of Monmouth at the Battle of Sedgemoor, others that they were noblemen dispossessed at the end of the Civil War. Some, recalling the brutality of the Danish invasions, say that the name is a corruption of Dane; yet others draw a link with a Scottish family exiled at the beginning of the seventeenth century; another, that they were descended from a Scottish servant named Doune who on the death

Jan Ridd's waterslide in Lank Combe.

of his master at Porlock fell on hard times. In 1901 one woman even claimed in the *West Somerset Free Press* to be 'Audrie Doune' and descended from Dounes exiled in 1620 who had settled in the Oare Valley. Towards the end of the century they were apparently invited to return to Scotland and left Exmoor for ever. Another 'exiled Scots' version states that they were headed by a Sir James Stewart

Malmsmead, once known as Moles Mead, at the heart of Doone Country and a good start point for exploring.

Reminding that this was brigand country, Robber's Bridge over Weir Water.

who on exile called himself Iain Ciar Duine, which locals corrupted to Ensor. The lands that Sir Ensor lost were those of Lorne in North Argyll which were sometimes called Lorna. In his Exmoor valley, Sir Ensor's sons became real outlaws and brigands while he, dreaming of recapturing his former wealth and title, kidnapped the daughter of the new lord to marry her off to his son Charles (Carver). To hide her identity she was given the name Lorna Doone.

Blackmore delightfully muddied the waters still further with the character of Tom Faggus, of North Molton, described by his cousin John Ridd, as 'a rough rude place at the end of Exmoor'. Tom had been a blacksmith – and there are photographs of his 'forge' there before it was knocked down in 1896 – but became a highwayman, according to Blackmore, after losing out in a dispute with Sir Robert Bampfylde, the lord of the manor (though in Tom's time the real lord was actually Sir Coplestone Bampfylde). Riding out on his faithful strawberry mare Winnie, he was a Robin Hood figure, robbing the rich and helping the poor. Unfortunately, there are no parish records of Tom, or his rough treatment, and he too, is almost certainly the stuff of legend.

Back to the Doones and another, theory, or red herring! According to C. Chadwyck Healey in *The History of Part of West Somerset* (1901):

> *... a venerable clergyman still living, who at the time was curate of Countisbury ... believes the real author of the Doone family was a fugitive from Sedgemoor fight, who only escaped hanging at the hands of Lord Jeffreys to carry on a series of petty depredations from a hovel on Exmoor. The old people used to tell Mr Thornton that the last two of the Doone family perished about the year 1800. An old man and his granddaughter set out to sing carols at Christmas and gather a few pence. They were found together in the snow, quite dead, on the road between Simonsbath and Challacombe.*

Thornton also reckoned to have been shown in 1848 'an antiquated gun with which an ancestor, so the farmer declared with great satisfaction, had shot a Doone who was prowling about his farmyard at night.' Chadwyck Healey felt these characters were more likely than any powerful body of outlaws. One wonders if he knew of another version which claimed that it was the Doones who had turned the old man and the little maid out into the snow. Perhaps he is right, though, because, as has been pointed out, the pugnacious Warden of the Forest at the time, James Boevey, was unlikely to have let a band of outlaws have their head for long. These only touch on the myriad theories.

Some writers, like Page and Edward Hutton, berated Blackmore for setting up visitors to come looking for the legendary valley, only to be disappointed that 'the real and the ideal do not coincide'. Then there was A.G. Bradley who was astonished by an encounter on Exmoor in 1870 when he was asked for directions to the Doone Valley, confessing that he and his companion had never heard of the book or the name. But he soon realised that the book would:

> *... mark the cleavage between the old Exmoor and the New as regards the British public. And that never again would it be possible for enlightened souls in the next county, indeed in any county, to say as they so often used to say to me: 'But where and what is Exmoor?'*

Long Combe Water.

Which in a way sums it up. No matter whether the Doones were real or no. Poor old Blackmore was ultimately irritated that he never again found the same success with any of his 15 subsequent novels, but to millions Lorna is a wonderful legacy and one hardly likely to be bettered in capturing the magic and mystery of Exmoor.

Moor amour

One wonders what the locals, who for aeons had farmed, fished, smuggled, swaled, hunted and harvested unheeded by the outside world, made of it. All of a sudden, in the eighteenth century Exmoor's 'filthy barren ground' was elevated to the cogniscenti's 'verdant vale' as the Romantic movement and war in Europe forced those for whom the Grand Tour was a kind of 'finishing school' to stay at home. They now appreciated the wildness and mystical qualities of nature – 'questing for a loveliness they could neither make nor control' as Presland put it in *Lynton and Lynmouth* (1918) – and though they stayed mainly round the coast and fringes, Exmoor certainly fitted the bill.

Locals found themselves joined by illustrious visitors, poets, writers and artists. J.M.W. Turner (whose parents hailed from South Molton), Gainsborough, Peter de Wint, William Payne and Nicholas Pocock, who died at Minehead, found their way and duly inspired, took their new vision of Exmoor to the outside world.

Turner when asked once about art, answered to the effect that it's all a bit of a rum do. Which probably summed up what the locals made of their new visitors. When Samuel Taylor Coleridge in 1797 came to live at Nether Stowey in the Quantocks, closely followed by William and Dorothy Wordsworth to nearby Alfoxden, they were reputedly shadowed by government agents on account of their 'revolutionary' ideas. Eventually the locals decided that Coleridge was probably a harmless chap who talked a lot, but Wordsworth was *'either a smuggler or a traitor, and means mischief. He never speaks to anyone, haunts lonely places, walks by moonlight [borne out by Dorothy's journals], and is always booing to himself.'*

It is unlikely they cared. They were ardent in their discovery of the Exmoor area, walking for miles, talking, and observing the country-side; they talked radical ideas, rejecting the 'artificiality' of English poetry hitherto and creating their own genre – and some of the greatest poems in the English language. *Lyrical Ballads*, which opened with the Ancient Mariner – devised on a walk to Lynton – and closed with Wordsworth's *Tintern Abbey*, is from this time. Dorothy Wordsworth in her journals records how the three of them had set off late one afternoon in mid-November to walk to Lynton (one wonders at the wisdom of their timing) by the coastal path. Having completed the first 8 miles to Watchet they put up there for the night. It was during this first leg of the journey, she said, that Wordsworth and Coleridge planned a ballad that would become the *Rhyme of the Ancient Mariner*. They worked out its 'powerful scheme' and sat down to write it together but Wordsworth then bowed out, leaving Coleridge to carry on with the idea.

Coleridge had also dreamt up, almost literally, the exotic Kubla Khan whilst staying at a farm near Culbone. It was conceived in best Sixties popstar style whilst emerging from an opium-induced stupor, claiming he had taken it for 'dysentry'. As he was writing it from memory, he is famously recorded as having been disturbed by a 'person from Porlock', after whose visit he could recall little more.

Coleridge and Robert Southey's wives were sisters and the latter too waxed lyrical; when weather-bound at the Old Ship Inn in Porlock one day he composed his sonnet on 'the verdant vale, so fair to sight'. Though his friends moved on – they still had the Lake District to immortalise – Southey did return in later life. Hazlitt, another friend and enthusiastic visitor, walked with him to the Valley of Rocks describing it as:

… bedded among precipices overhanging the sea, with rocky cavern beneath, into which the waves dash and where the seagull forever wheels its screaming flight.

Southey and Hazlitt were much impressed with the Valley of Rocks.

Another rather wild genius who flitted in moth-like to the flame of Exmoor's untamed shores, if not moor, was Shelley. Already dubbed 'mad Shelley' for his independent spirit, he had quarrelled with his family and relinquished his inheritance after eloping with sixteen-year-old Harriet Westbrook. Wandering from here to there, in 1812 they pitched up in Lynmouth, a favourite haunt of these new Romantics, set up a commune of 'like spirits' and wrote *Queen Mab* before flitting off again.

It is perhaps Exmoor's good fortune that they did move on, to immortalise the Lakes, whilst leaving this moor to be a hidden gem. The moor itself was still fairly inaccessible, except around the coasts where the new fashion for sea bathing and the gradual dawning of tourism brought people to the coastal watering places like Lynton and Ilfracombe. Exmoor got on with it, at least until *Lorna*, whilst continuing to be home to and inspire, artists, authors, poets, music makers, hymn-writers and craftspeople. It is said to be the inspiration for the first hymn most of us learn, 'All Things Bright and Beautiful', and anyone hearing a class of infants singing it must feel Exmoor could have no better tribute. The tinker poet Dicky Slader also wrote many hymns and Yankee Jack, who retired to Watchet, collected many folk songs from the area as well as his famous sea chanteys, later documented by Cecil Sharp.

In the footsteps of Turner and Gainsborough came artists like William Widgery, born in North Molton, whose romantic style is still sought after, David Cox, William J. Muller, and J.W. North. Itinerate clergyman the Reverend John Swete (originally called Tripe!) visited Exmoor on his travels all over the West Country and left an invaluable legacy of hundreds of watercolours. He appeared to anticipate the impact of the forthcoming Industrial Revolution and records a rural landscape unspoilt by roads or railways where life went on as it had for centuries. His views of Exmoor are all the more fascinating because they show a landscape still recognisable today unlike, for instance, Torbay.

Edward Cooke was one of the greatest marine artists of the nineteenth century and a passionate plantsman. He painted and sketched on several visits, at Dunster, Lynmouth, Porlock Weir and Blue Anchor among others, and collected ferns near Watersmeet. In recent years his work has commanded high prices.

Another group, who came to the fore around the end of the nineteenth century, memorably combined their appreciation of Exmoor with a celebration of the hunting scene: Cecil Aldin, Sir Alfred Munnings, Lionel Edwards, whose first exhibition was at Porlock Parish Rooms, New Zealander H.S. Power and more recently Michael Lyne and Peter Biegel. It is interesting that though Exmoor has been much painted, examples can be very hard to find, having been dispersed around the country and abroad. There is no slackening of demand for contemporary works. Ken Hildrew, whose home and studio are in North Molton, was contacted by a gallery owner in the USA who, having checked whether 'Landacre Bridge was still there' said he could sell as many paintings of Exmoor as Ken could supply. They are also much in demand here as Ken and many other artists inspired to depict the moor today, John Hoar, Colin Allbrook, Donald Ayers, Lionel Aggett, Ken Doughty, Sheila Ferguson, Anne le Bas among them, will testify.

Blackmore certainly did not have the last word on writing about Exmoor. John Fortescue, Richard Jefferies, F.J. Snell, Henry Williamson, whose classic *Tarka the Otter* was partly set on the moor; all are much-loved and unsurpassed. Williamson in Tarka evokes the moor thus:

Exmoor is the high country of the winds, which are to the falcons and the hawks: clothed by whortleberry bushes and lichens and ferns and mossed trees in goyals, which are to the foxes, the badgers and the Red Deer: served by rain clouds and drained by rock-littered streams, which are to the otters.

Jefferies, though Wiltshire-born, visited Exmoor in 1883, and was taken out on the moor and taught about the red deer by Fred Heal,

North Molton after Rain.

Ken Hildrew

a farming and hunting man of the time. The book of the same name, *Red Deer*, published the following year, became a classic of its kind. In it he created, in his distinctive prose that managed to combine fact with sensitive observation and almost poetic description, a splendid record of of the life cycle and habits of the red deer and his observations regarding hunting at the time. He also records an Exmoor with few fences, few visitors, less of the wild land reclaimed and made much of the friendliness and courtesy of Exmoor folk to those like himself who did visit:

> …'*every man according to his station nods his head or touches his hat, and no one passes another without saluting …*'

Today, that is one of the aspects of Exmoor that has not changed. R.F. Delderfield, educated for a time at West Buckland School, immortalised it in *To Serve Them All My Days*. Journalists such as Herbert Kille and Jack Hurley, in their chronicling of the moor and its people, are now synonymous with Exmoor. Former poet Laureate Ted Hughes lived not far away and set two of his poems on the moor. Contemporary writers living and working on the moor include Margaret Drabble, Ranulph Fiennes, Hazel Holt and Michael Holroyd. But some of the most powerful evocations of Exmoor come from the pen of Hope Bourne whose simple, honest records of her self-sufficient life on the moor near Withypool, are unique:

> *There will be days … when the bronze-budded beech suddenly bursts into such a glory of green as no mortal mind could imagine of itself, translucent golden green like a million, million green butterflies trembling in the breeze. …days when the heather is come, its purple glory spread across the hills, the soft wind blowing its scent to me, sweet and heady like a mixture of honey and wine in the sun … days when the fern will turn to sheets of copper and the beech to flame and the oaks to beaten gold, and I will be bewildered trying to catch the colours with my paintbox before leaves come down for winter-time.*

Porlock shingle ridge and groynes.   Sheila Wilkinson

Chapter 14

❧

MYTH AND MYTHOLOGY

Perhaps it is not surprising that a place with as many wild, hidden corners as Exmoor should be a cauldron of myth and legend and Exmoor has more than its fair share, enough to fill volumes. Pixies, the Devil, ghostly white doves and accursed cannonballs, are just a few of the fascinating tales.

A flaming autumn morning at Tarr Steps is mirrored Monet-like in a Barle flowing sedately after a dry summer. Hard to imagine the fury of water that displaced the ancient stone bridge in the terrible storm of 1952. Hard too, to

Check that the Devil isn't sunbathing before crossing Tarr Steps.

D. Coxon

fathom, just how it got there in ancient times. However many times you visit it, the clapper bridge at Tarr Steps holds enduring fascination and mystery. At 180ft long, with 17 stone spans, its largest single stone is 8ft 6in by 5ft wide. No one knows where the stones come from because there is no similar rock in the area. No one really knows why it is there though it links two ridgeways that were Bronze

Age burial grounds of around 3000 years ago. There is no cement or binding material to hold the stones in place and of course they have not always remained so though it took extreme weather to dislodge them in both 1952 and 1941/42.

Both times they were replaced by Royal Engineers but the other mystery, like Stonehenge, is how the stones, not from close by, were heaved into position in the first place by people with no machinery at their disposal. One legend makes a cracking yarn. It tells that the bridge was built in a single night by the Devil (who else?) who liked to sunbathe there, and when a cat presumed to venture across it, it was instantly torn to pieces. This was all too much for the rector of Hawkridge, just up the hill, who besides seeing his parishioners in peril, thought the Devil had had enough of his own way so he set off across, stopping and turning to exchange compliments 'more forcible than polite' with Master Devil on the bank. The Devil called the parson a 'black crow' to which he replied that he was not 'blacker than the Devil'. He made it safely to the other side.

The woodland around Tarr Steps has been designated a National Nature Reserve in the year of the National Park's fiftieth anniversary. Though it can get a little congested, this beautiful and magical place is always worth a visit.

The Devil seems to have been kept busy on Exmoor being credited with creating the Punchbowl on Winsford Hill, the Whitstones on Porlock Hill and Rugged Jack in the Valley of Rocks. The latter was supposed to be the leader of a drunken rabble who made merry on the sabbath but did not recognise the Devil when he tried to join in so he turned them all to stone. The Whitstones, two ancient stones near the top of Porlock Hill, were said to have been thrown in a contest between the Devil and a giant! Another tale reckons that Jesus visited with Joseph of Arimathea. When they needed to find water Joseph sank his staff into the ground and Sisters' Fountain spring at Glenthorne issued forth.

The Whitstones, used in a contest between the Devil and a giant?

Colourful customs steeped in legend and surviving to the present day include the ceremony of the Hunting of the Earl of Rone at Combe Martin (strangely involving much pub visiting!), wassailing on old Twelfth Night at Carhampton and the Minehead Hobby Horse on May Day.

White Dove of Bardon

The ancient manor house of Bardon hidden away in the north-east corner of Exmoor, in the parish of old Cleeve, is an intensely mysterious place, unfortunately not open to the public, but has earned a place in Exmoor's folklore that is worth the telling. Like all such tales, versions differ but this is one of the author's favourites, weaving as it does history, high intrigue and legend.

When in 1587 the executioner's axe was about to fall on the slender neck of Mary Queen of Scots, Elizabeth I, is said to have mused, 'Can

Rugged Jack in the Valley of Rocks.   D. Coxon

Bardon, home of the White Dove legend and many more. D. Coxon

I slay the dove which pursued by a falcon has flown to me for help?' More than 200 years later in 1836, at faraway Bardon, its master Robert Leigh was told of an attic window that had been broken. It was repaired but days later was broken again, according to the servants, by a white dove that had repeatedly flown against the pane. Its action was to unseal a secret that had lain long hidden. Leigh investigated and in the attic found an old box. In it were State papers that appeared to have nothing to do with this remote country house, implicating Mary Queen of Scots in the Babington Plot against her cousin Queen Elizabeth I, though they also contained her strenuous denials. One bundle of papers was the whole prosecution case in the plot, which had mysteriously vanished from London after the trial, clearly stating that the testimony of three servants against Mary had been extracted under threat of the rack.

The papers were important enough to be acquired by the British Museum in 1970 but what were they doing at Bardon anyway? They were found in a container known as the 'Throckmorton' box. A former Leigh of Bardon had been lawyer to Sir Robert Throckmorton, who owned a property nearby and across the moor

at Molland where his descendants are known today. It was a name writ large, like that of Babington, in the intrigue and plotting that surrounded Elizabeth's tenure of the throne. One, Francis, was tortured and executed at Tyburn for his part in a plot to assassinate Elizabeth. His brother Thomas settled in Paris as an agent of Mary, while a relative, Nicholas, though a Protestant, is said to have supported Mary's cause and been much taken with her considerable charm. So it is credible that somehow the papers ended up with the Throckmortons who passed them into the safe keeping of the family lawyers at Bardon. Another facet of the story is why an obscure country lawyer should have been made the gift of Bardon by the Queen in the first place. Though not a man about court, Leigh was closely linked with a man called Scudamore who in turn was Walsingham's man – the head of Elizabeth's Secret Service. We know that Mary was long a thorn in Elizabeth's side with her unswerving belief that she should be on the throne. But the Babington Plot letter that led to trial was part of the ruthless conspiracy-busting machine of Elizabeth's ministers Burleigh and Walsingham. It had emanated from the latter's office and was a forgery. No doubt Mary's spirit — the white dove – could not rest until the world knew. And perhaps this was the service that Robert Leigh had done for Elizabeth, in harbouring papers that could have exposed the prosecution case.

It is easy to see how the white dove, especially after Elizabeth's curious comment, became interpreted as being the spirit of Mary – white to denote her innocence, anxious that somehow her written denials should one day be seen by the world. Quite why she waited so long begs an answer but the story goes that afterwards the dove was never seen again at the window.

Bardon's intrigue doesn't end there. Even today ghostly tales abound, curiously for a house that remained a stronghold of lawyers. One of the Leighs is supposed to have walked the grounds, carrying a head (not his own) under his arm, while at other times the crunch of wheels and hooves sound on the gravel drive. Other tales tell of a white-haired lady of 'sorrowful countenance' gliding through the rooms in a dress of rustling silk, and of plaintive music being played on a spinet or harpsichord. A black dog was also said to appear before the death of a member of the family. *West Somerset Free Press* journalist Clement Kille was told that the Bardon spirits had been exorcised by seven parsons with bell, book and candle in the nineteenth century. But it appears their mission failed as the dog appeared again many years later.

Bardon still exudes an air of mystery and visitors still attest to its spooky atmosphere. Both were used to good effect in a film about the life of Samuel Taylor Coleridge (though ironically it appears as Wordsworth's Dove Cottage in the Lake District). When the author visited, the whole aura of one room was dominated by a floor-to-ceiling glass case containing a ferocious wild cat. 'Trophy of an ancestor,' I inquired? No I bought it in an antiques shop in Watchet,' laughed the owner.

Drake's cannonball

Not far away from Bardon, near Monksilver, stands the Elizabethan manor house, built, or rebuilt, in 1580 by George Sydenham, father-in-law to be to Sir Francis Drake, whose presence is still very much felt there. Restoration of the Grade 1 listed Combe Sydenham house and 500-acre estate has been something of a magnificent obsession, spanning almost forty years, for the present owner William Theed. Nowhere is this seen to better effect than in the lovingly restored and eerily beautiful court room where lies about the only thing that did not need any work – a 100lb meteorite known as Drake's cannonball and legend has it, a sign from heaven in the most romantic of tales. Like all the best legends, versions vary, as recounted by former owners, local journalists and one of Exmoor's best-loved writers Richard Jefferies. But at its heart it is a wonderful story about the enduring love between Sir Francis Drake and his second wife Elizabeth Sydenham. After the death of his first wife Mary, Drake wooed Elizabeth, tall, beautiful and half her suitor's age. Bold adventurer and Queen's favourite though he was, Drake was also, in

Combe Sydenham, with limewashed exterior, using local pigments, home of Drake's cannonball and resident ghosts. D. Coxon

the eyes of Elizabeth's parents, a stocky, middle-aged man of humble origins who could not be relied upon to stay at home. But though they cautioned against the liaison, love won the day and in 1585 Elizabeth married Drake in nearby Monksilver church.

She was soon back at Combe Sydenham, awaiting Drake's return from sea and as the months became years, it seemed that Drake must have been lost. The law or tradition of the time was that if after seven years a husband and wife had heard nothing of each other, either was free to remarry, whether or not the other's death was confirmed. Always believing that Drake was still alive, Elizabeth, prepared to marry a wealthy young suitor from nearby Williton when the seven years were up. Still no news came, time ran out and Elizabeth, still sure, even up to her wedding morning that Drake was alive, prayed for some sign to prevent the marriage. It looked hopeless as she descended the stairs in her bridal finery and stepped forward to take the hand of her groom. As their hands clasped the 'cannonball' rolled or – if you prefer – hurtled between them with a blinding flash and thunderous roar. It was Elizabeth's sign. Sure enough, Drake had arrived in Plymouth and the next day (somewhat swiftly) arrived at Combe Sydenham and whisked her away, leaving the famous 'cannonball'.

In fact the ball is far too heavy to have been fired from any of Drake's cannons, even if it could have travelled all the way to North Somerset, and according to both local and expert opinion, is a meteorite. Both it and Drake have since acquired their own individual folklore. According to one story, the ball settled itself in the hall at Combe Sydenham and if moved would always return to the same spot:, another that if the ball was carried away and thrown in the deepest of Combe Sydenham's ponds it would always be back in the hall at the break of day. Somewhat confounding these tales, the ball was in fact removed for a time to Taunton museum and failed to find its own way back. But it is said to bring luck to anyone who touches it and a curse if anyone removes it. Supposedly Combe Sydenham was indeed hit by disaster and declining fortunes when it was away. Mr Theed says that when experts arrived to examine it in situ, they 'got their bottoms in the air and stated that it was one of only 23 known meteorites in the country and only one other iron one and they thought this was iron but would have to take it away to find out. I told them that there was a curse on it and that when it had been taken away before, everything had fallen to pieces so I just didn't want to know.' Whatever its origin, there is no other explanation for how it got there. The ball now sits in front of a fireplace in the court room and, dear reader, the author has touched it. Combe Sydenham is a magical place but sadly, she has not noticed any great luck befalling! Like Bardon, Combe Sydenham holds more than one mystery: there are tales of the ghost of Sir George appearing, along with a Cavalier wearing a cloak and Spanish hat and a coach drawn by horses shod with silver haunting the grounds.

Exmoor beast

A beastly subject to tackle this one! After a spate of activity and interest in the eighties, things have seemed quieter in recent years. Yet according to the British Big Cats Society, at time of writing sightings of 'beasts' in the South West rose by 61 per cent in 2003–2004. And almost everyone living round the moor has amongst their acquaintances someone who claims to have seen it. Reports began in the late 1970s of sightings of a large cat-like animal, either black or dark grey, with a long tail, standing low to the ground but able to jump 6ft-high fences. Sheep have also been attacked over the years, the markings left on them indicate something far worse than a dog to blame. A black panther, puma, leopard or lynx have been suggested, or some hybrid produced by an escaped black puma mating with another feline and establishing a breeding colony.

Mary Rawle, who has lived on Exmoor all her life and farmed it for over fifty years, still recalls vividly her sighting of the 'beast' – though as she says, it is only an animal – on North Molton Common, near her own farm.

Out early in the morning on horseback and with her two dogs at her feet, all was quiet as some deer rose up in front of her. 'I had climbed above a rather boggy bit and then looked into a drier part of the bog and it must have seen me before I saw it – what I would describe as a pert cat-like face, pricky ears, looking back at me. Suddenly it got up and I could see that it had the most wonderful sleek black coat, but with a white blaze, then it bounded away, not running like a dog but bounding. I suppose I was about a couple of hundred yards away. I had never seen an animal like it.'

Though she had no more such close encounters, Mary recalls smelling it twice – 'an unmistakable stink' – and like so many others round about found lost lambs that were eaten out from the hind legs round to the innards in a way that she had never come across before. On one occasion she saw something scudding along a path, on another heard a strange noise whereupon she found her dogs had already fled, and yet another time found a field of young bullocks so spooked that they did not want their food.

Put alongside of sightings by neighbours, Mary feels that her particular 'beast' seemed to move over a distinctive territory, up from Whitechapel, Twitchen to Sandyway and back, the way of the old tramline through the Mole Valley.

At various times in the eighties, sheep killings and sightings were serious enough for extra help to be called in. In 1983, after a spate of sheep killings 50 men on horseback, supported by day by Torrington Foot Beagles and a local police helicopter searched Exmoor for the elusive creature. The following month Marines with night-vision equipment began a week-long operation – to no avail – and over the years killings and sightings have occurred sporadically. Inevitably some theorise that this points to a supernatural being. In 1988 Marines called in by the Ministry of Agriculture – who had always dismissed reports of 'Alien Big Cats' – again tried to corner the creature which was reported to be in a barn and surrounded. When they went in it had gone.

Mary felt that there was something of the comic about grown men in camouflage, hiding behind gorse bushes, when any 'beast' would have smelt them long before and fled. Her own feeling is that there may be a link with military presence on the moor in the war, accompanied by mascots – and that her 'beast' is probably long dead. As she points out, winters too are nothing like as harsh as they used to be, which would mean any beast could survive on a plentiful supply of pheasants.

Sightings have continued though some claim the beast has extended its roamings throughout Somerset. Whatever the truth, the 'beast' has certainly become part of the folklore of Exmoor.

And so to pixies … In *Lorna Doone* Marwood de Winchelhase says: 'No dog, no man is the rule about here when it comes to coppice work, there is not a man who dare work here without a dog to scare the pixies.' There are too many pixie tales to relate here but perhaps the most popular theory to 'explain' the long-held belief of their existence is that they were a people conquered but not destroyed by Celtic incomers, who long afterwards lived in scattered communities in wild places. Being small of stature and quick of movement, they lived in low turf-covered huts and used their knowledge of secret ways to flit about. F.J. Snell more prosaically reckoned it to be a tale put about by smugglers for their own ends. Whatever – the name lives on in many places such as Pixie Rocks in Challacombe Glen, Pixie Copse in Bury and according to the 3rd Earl of Carnarvon, Pixton Park originally meant Pixie Town.

Exmoor beast.   Matthew Coxon, aged twelve

Chapter 15

WHERE NOW?

There is a saying that if you hear the end of the world is nigh, move to Porlock as everything happens here fifty years late. It could as easily apply to the whole of Exmoor for if anything defines Exmoor, it is its aura of being out of time. As it slipped into the twentieth century it's doubtful whether anyone really noticed; through war and devastating flood, they soldiered on. Changes were slow in coming; electricity did not come to the villages until several years after the Second World War had ended.

Only true Exmoor folk, born and bred, many of whom feel that their home country is now gone for ever, can know when 'yesterday ended' as Hazel Eardley-Wilmot puts it. She dates it quite precisely to the early 1950s when grants to help put the farmers back on their feet after the war changed the landscape almost overnight. It would also of course in 1954 see Exmoor's designation as a National Park. The ancient boundary road along Fyldon Ridge and on past Kinsford Cross was not modernised until after the Lynmouth disaster -- with money available from the oversubscribed relief fund. But those who were around then and are still, would each have a different story, a different Exmoor; their memories and thoughts are the remit of another book. Mary Rawle, a friend of Hazel's, who has farmed on Exmoor for over fifty years, told the author sadly that it was after the war that things changed so radically and irrevocably

New dawn over Exmoor.

that she likens it to the Highland Clearances. As far as Mary is concerned the death of Exmoor's small-farming way of life is a tragedy because as she puts it, 'one day the world may well be hungry but millions of productive acres have been lost'.

For many it was a hard life but one that was accepted. People walked huge distances and made do with very little though according to Mary it was a good life. But farmer's wife Norma Huxtable tells how it was the need for a new pair of stockings and the response of her husband, the farmer/husband/boss, that she had had a new pair at Christmas, that led her into bed and breakfast – before diversification was even a word.

Thus whilst very much living the traditional role, Norma subtly found herself embracing inevitable change. Yet even in the late 1980s when we came to Exmoor, we would watch an old-world 'tableau', fascinated, every Saturday night at the Poltimore Arms at Yarde Down. On the dot would appear a middle-aged farmer, with his wife and son. Drinks ordered, he would enjoy his alone or perhaps talking to other customers; his wife and son were clearly expected to be seen – barely – and not heard. The Poltimore itself is one of those places where you can still fancy that time has stood still, especially when the lights black out as they do regularly, then are restored, because it is still on generator. Farmers and riding folk chinwag in their Exmoor burr and visitors are made truly welcome.

Britain's National Parks came about, albeit after decades of pressure and wrangling, precisely because of the worries of conservation and amenity organisations that Britain's beautiful and unspoilt countryside would be swallowed up for ever by the encroachment of man and machine. They are charged with the dual aims of conserving and enhancing the natural beauty, wildlife and cultural heritage, and promoting opportunities for the understanding and enjoyment of their special qualities. Exmoor certainly offered an abundance of the latter, too precious to be left to the vicissitudes of a fast-changing world: the natural beauty of its moorland, wooded combes and

Exuding unruffled atmosphere in afternoon sunshine – but for how long?

valleys, coastal cliffs and woodland, Red Deer, ponies and other rare flora and fauna; historical features ranging from Bronze Age barrows and packhorse bridges to thatched cottages and beautiful churches; and its fresh air and open spaces, bridleways and tracks for riding and walking, rivers for fishing and its literary and artistic associations.

But the area was designated amid controversy; both Devon and Somerset County Councils and many inhabitants and landowners were hostile to what they saw as unwarranted outside control. What was the trickiest of briefs for any organisation was all the more precarious on Exmoor because it is so small: small changes have far-reaching effects, and in the same way too big an influx of visitors, especially to 'honeypot' spots, rapidly puts under threat the beauty they have come to enjoy. Controversy and opposition, often more to policies than the people on the ground charged with the task, would never be far away. When in 1959 the Forestry Commission planned to plant conifers on The Chains, the opposition came from a small group who would become the Exmoor Society. They have since worked tirelessly to preserve the Exmoor they know and love, at times in conflict with the National Park, but seeking wherever possible to work with them and bodies such as the Council for Protection of Rural England.

With the twenty-first century well underway, outwardly Exmoor looks as unruffled and beautiful as ever – for all the world as if those who feared for Exmoor were just doom and gloom merchants. But, of course we know that in the past ten years it has had to weather BSE, foot and mouth, a crisis in farming generally with bureaucracy

End of another glorious day.

and changing policies from the EC and collapsing prices at the farm gate: the problem of second home-owners and high house prices beyond the reach of young locals, and the threat of a ban on hunting with dogs, which many see as the lifeblood of Exmoor. Through it all, farmers, locals, business and bodies such as the National Park, the Exmoor Society, the National Trust, English Nature and English Heritage and others have battled to keep Exmoor special. Visitors play their part too, making voluntary contributions or paying a levy in B & Bs, hotels and restaurants to fund projects to make the countryside more accessible, while also lessening the inevitable wear and tear on paths and bridleways.

Farming is no longer the dominant force and main employer, having given way to service industries and tourism – but it does survive thanks to a characteristic resilience of many and adaptability of those who have diversified. Some have embraced the organic movement with aplomb, tapping in to growing demand for top-quality, sourced food, and establishing schemes for direct supply and marketing. Other diversifications include game crops, deer farming, fish farming and even alpacas, ostrich and a vineyard. Exmoor National Park Authority pioneered management agreement schemes to compensate landowners and farmers for loss of income from implementing conservation measures. It has also tried to plug the gaps in the plethora of Government and other schemes, to help Exmoor's small and hard-pressed hill farms. Farmers for their part bought the markets at Barnstaple, Cutcombe and Blackmoor Gate, in a bold bid to ensure a future. But when the price of wool is hardly greater than the cost of shearing and lamb prices likewise, it is no surprise that some simply quit. One such, who first opted to combine it with a 'diversification' crop – willow – urged on by Government 'renewable energy' schemes – quit in disillusionment as the goalposts continually changed. Pre-foot and mouth he predicted to the author that within twenty years the countryside would be just one big theme park. Oh dear. We can only hope that the determination and efforts of all concerned against such a grim prospect will prevail.

If tourism is now the main cashcrop there is an upside, as well as that of directly provided employment. More and more people are engaged in keeping traditional crafts and customs alive and providing local and distinctive food; artists and craftspeople too take inspiration from their surroundings: painters, writers, furniture makers, weavers, glass makers, paper makers, wrought iron, pottery, jewellery, Exmoor has them all. Musical events and festivals, too which as well as all 'making work for the working man to do' can only enrich Exmoor as a living landscape. No doubt if we could step back to the days that seem so rose tinted now we would find that the balance was ever shifting.

In 1999 on the anniversary of the National Park movement Prince Charles flagged up the 'difficult balance in engaging the interests of the local communities, whose own activities play such an important part in maintaining the landscape and wildlife.' He also drew attention to the fact that only 10 per cent of England and Wales is National Park and pondered the fate of the many special areas of countryside which did not enjoy such protection. Certainly the work of Exmoor National Park Authority, carried out by a dedicated band of experts and volunteers, is now so wide ranging it is hard to see how Exmoor could just be left to muddle through without it. Look at some of the initiatives of just the past year: opening of the restored historic sawmill at Simonsbath; work to investigate and conserve Devon's thatched buildings; archaeological digs to investigate Roman iron production at Brayford and Mesolithic remains at Hawkcombe; a survey of Exmoor's breeding birds; a major heathland restoration project at Haddon Hill; moves to tackle the huge problem of affordable housing as prices rocket; and many other projects, as well as its programme of more than 100 guided walks. More than 7000 people were carried on the Snowdrop Park and Ride Scheme, achieving its aim of minimising environmental damage whilst bringing a much needed boost to the local economy at a grim time of year.

Of course, woven through the heart of Exmoor landscape is still the riding culture and hunting that has endured for some thousand years, but at the time of writing this is teetering on the brink. Hunting itself may only involve a relatively small number of residents but so many businesses and many other equestrian events are irrevocably entwined: point-to-points, gymkhanas, horse shows, fairs and festivals. There is also the stance of the majority of farmers that the deer, which undoubtedly do much damage to their crops, are tolerated and indeed thrive because of the balance established by hunting. Perhaps the debate could hardly be better summed up than as stated by the Exmoor Society: 'Our members have diverse opinions and the Society has always adopted a neutral stance on the merits and demerits of hunting, while expressing concern about the conservation of Exmoor's historic and irreplaceable herd of red deer.' In its submission to the Minister of Rural Affairs, it says: 'At the heart of this submission is the Society's conviction that it is simply not a valid option to do nothing except to make it illegal to hunt red deer on horseback with dogs. Such a policy could result in the rapid degrading of the red deer herd.' They point out that the herd of some 2500 deer currently exists in an eco-system in harmonious balance and cite how in the Second World War when the herd was neglected it came close to extinction.

Whatever your views it is hard to see how the character of Exmoor could survive a ban that would strike at the equestrian culture, related business and farming in one single hammer blow.

But as we have seen the living has never been easy on Exmoor, any more than it is an easy place to know. Perhaps its most amazing enigma is that for all this, you can still feel its spirit, still escape into another world – and then discover another.

Exmoor, riding capital of England.

A flash and then gone, hopefully not for ever.

Chapter 16

EXPLORING EXMOOR

Walk the paths, drive the lanes of Exmoor and for much of the time you will be passing the same way as our ancestors, millennia before there were marked routes. They would find their way by means of known landmarks, barrows perhaps, using ridgeways, guiding strangers through their land. Now a reasonably fit person can traverse the Park in a day yet still many pass by or pass through, when by looking just a little further, or merely stopping to stare, they could not fail to go away refreshed and enriched.

The aim of this evocation of Exmoor has been to convey something of the atmosphere of this place that was born in the clouds of pre-history, perhaps to convey another Exmoor you did not know before, which makes it impossible to provide a one-size-fits-all guide: far better the personal journey anyway and the thrill of discovering for yourself. If you really cannot leave the

An early-morning balloon launch from Landacre Bridge.
D. Coxon

car, then Exmoor will not disappoint On a winter's day when I had walked along past Cow Castle, a mini-bus of senior citizens had stopped to stare and were rewarded with a spectacular rainbow. But if you are able to walk even a short distance off the beaten track, do and you will not be disappointed.

No one is likely to forget their first sighting of Castle Rock plunging to the sea at the Valley of Rocks when rounding a bend in the path from North Hill, a stunning walk in itself with scree and tottering rock pinnacles above and stomach-churning drop to the sea below on your right. If you walk back by road, the whole spectacular journey is only 2 miles. Or scramble out over Hollerday Hill, starting from behind Lynton's Town Hall, for a wonderful variation. The Valley of Rocks is part of the South West Coast path, the longest of the National Trails of England and Wales and includes 34 miles (54km) of Exmoor's coastline. It is also a 'do-able' chunk whereas the whole section of trail involves some hamstring-testing climbs so it is best to be sure of your capabilities.

Many people like their walks to be mapped out for them or to be guaranteed of a teashop or pub somewhere en route and there are many excellent guides, from leaflet to book, available in shops all over Exmoor and Visitor Centres. There is also an ongoing programme of specialised walks, boat trips, cycling and riding events, accompanied by National Park guides, to help you find out more about anything from bats to barrows. But equally, Exmoor has over 600 miles (1000 kilometres) of public rights of way, covering moorland, woods, valleys and the coast, offering everything from the toughest hike to a gentle wander. This network of routes, which includes three major trails – the Two Moors Way, the Tarka Trail and the South West Coast path – is clearly marked on OS maps and by their own waymarks on the moor itself. If you prefer to do it your way, plan your own routes and the possibilities are endless. It has been observed that the Two Moors Way can be like the walker's M25 in high season, so if it is wilderness you crave, plan in your own variations if possible. Be aware though that 75 per cent of Exmoor is actually privately owned at present and is accessible as a matter of goodwill. Shoulsbury Castle proved suitably impregnable when the author set out to check out the wonderful views described in a number of books. It is best to keep to rights of way marked on OS maps and the colour-coded waymarks which indicate permission to roam from landowners. Yellow routes are for walkers only, blue routes can also be used by cyclists and riders; red routes are for motor vehicles; white markers indicate 'permissive' routes where access permission has been granted by landowners. Some walks are linked with bus routes and any occasion when you can travel this way rather than by car has to be beneficial to all who wish to enjoy the tranquillity of the moor. Snowdrop Valley was once very much a local secret, until its popularity with visitors travelling by car put it under threat. Since the early 1980s the National Park Authority has worked with local landowners to conserve the snowdrops and the road is now closed at busy times, with a park and ride scheme taking visitors to the valley from Wheddon Cross.

Above: *Winter walking from Hoccombe Water down into Doone Country.*

Below: *Ladies' Mile near Hunter's Inn, a lovely woodland walk.*

Above left: *Just a few steps further at Watersmeet brings you on another spectacular waterfall.*

Above: *A walk accessible for the disabled at Webber's Post.*

Left: *Beware adders – it is rare for anyone to be bitten by Britain's only poisonous snake as they prefer to slide away unnoticed – but if you should inadvertently step on one, or your dog is too interested, they will strike!*

On the Macmillan Way West dropping down towards Wootton Courtenay.

It is fitting in this home of our most ancient horse that riding and Exmoor go hand in hand and indeed it is known as the 'riding playground of England'. An abiding personal memory is of a quiet moment at Tarr Steps one morning before heading back to city stresses, when two riders splashed through with a greeting. When we can do that on a Monday morning we vowed, we will have got it right. That moment brought us to Exmoor for good.

Certainly, with over 400 miles (645km) of bridleways, there is no finer way of seeing all the scenery that the moor, valleys and woodlands have to offer. Nor do you have to be an experienced horseperson. Riding centres across the area offer something for everyone from novice to the most experienced, with facilities for hunting, hacking, and trekking; some hotels and guest houses also offer stabling for your horse and complete riding holidays are available. As well as having that extra height on the scene there is the added beauty of taking in more terrain in less time, yet always unhurried. A circular 12-mile ride over the moorland heathers around Doone Country, starting from the cattle grid just before Alderman's Barrow, takes in the site of Frederic Knight's ill-fated tramline from Simonsbath to Porlock Weir; the ruins of Larkbarrow, a former Royal Forest farmstead destroyed by artillery practice in the Second World War; East Pinford Stell, the name for a stone-built sheep shelter, brought to Exmoor by the Scottish shepherds; whortleberries, perhaps; a stone setting; the ruins of Badgworthy and a stone memorial to Blackmore, and Oare Church. Quite a ride through history!

There are, of course, many other ways of experiencing the Exmoor effect, through enjoyment of more specialist recreations: cycling, watersports, shooting and fishing, are all well established and offer a different perpective. Cycling – despite the contours – is increasingly popular, not just for those who see hills as a challenge, but by families who just want to enjoy the scenery. Dunster Woods offers three trails, all starting at Nutcombe Bottom, for various abilities. Part of the National Millennium Cycle Route passes along the southern edge of the moor, with fabulous views, quiet, level roads (after an initial climb!) and organically shaped wooden seats for a roadside rest. You can even ride over Dunkery – and plenty do – for extra Exmoor effect!

The view from the sea is yet another perspective on Exmoor and the only way to see seabirds, ancient woodland, towering cliffs and smugglers' haunts; there are regular trips from Lynmouth. There are no sandy beaches within the National Park boundary though there are several just along the coast but bathing is possible, if bracing, at Lee Bay and Combe Martin. Others, such as Sillery Sands, Woody Bay, Wringcliff Bay, Heddon's Mouth and Wild Pear Beach, may involve quite a scramble and the latter is also good for fossil spotters. Sailing is popular, if limited by the tidal range of the Bristol Channel; surfing, though more concentrated on the North Devon Atlantic beaches, moves to Lynmouth when conditions dictate. The little harbour is also popular for surf boarding, surf canoeing and wave skiing and jet skiing. Wimbleball Lake is ideal for safe sailing and also offers board sailing and canoeing. Kayaking takes place, by permit only, on rivers such as the Barle and East Lyn, whilst sea kayaking against the backdrop of towering cliffs has got to be the ultimate way to take in their grandeur but is a specialist activity best done in a group.

If anywhere could be said to be the image of 'under an English heaven' it is Exmoor and nowhere will you find that essence of Englishness and traditional ways more than at one of the small agricultural shows, like Dunster or Exford. Here you can see traditional Exmoor breeds, see Exmoor ponies at Exford Show, watch pony clubgames and other equestrian events, sample delicious local products and crafts, and mingle with Exmoor folk. Here, for a little while at least, you can take comfort that the English countryside – and Exmoor in particular – is not yet just another theme park. You can enjoy the crowd here all the more knowing that soon you can be alone again amid wildness as far as the eye can see, broken only by a wind-blasted tree.

Anti-clockwise, starting top right:
Terrier racing.

*Up and over – point-to-pointing is one of
Exmoor's favourite sporting fixtures.*

Fly fishing.

Antlers and bouncy castles – where else but Exmoor?

Rally driving.

Clockwise, starting top left:

Scrambling.

Sailing on Wimbleball.

Mountain biking.

Vintage cars.

Porlock Horse Show.

Flying the kite for Exmoor.

Pleasure boats bobbing in Lynmouth harbour.

Some Exmoor Sites to Visit:

Allerford – Chocolate-box Domesday hamlet on the Holnicote estate, in Selworthy parish, with fifteenth-century packhorse bridge over Aller Brook. Thatched old school is now home to the West Somerset Museum of Rural Life.

Thatched old schoolhouse, Allerford.

Barbrook – Hamlet on West Lyn upstream from Lynton and Lynmouth, with memorial to those who lost their lives in the 1952 flood disaster, and rebuilt bridge.

Blackmoor Gate – Centuries-old crossing of tracks along ancient ridgeway from Exmoor to sea, now a crossroads of A39 and A399. Until mid-1800s open moorland ran to the east of the road, with a gate onto the moor. It is named after R.D. Blackmore's family who owned much of the land around Parracombe.

Lynch Chapel.

Bossington – Ancient and attractive hamlet dating to Saxon times, also part of Holnicote Estate. Lovely walks along the Coast Path to Hurlstone Point and Porlock Marsh, and a glorious view from Bossington Hill. Nearby is the medieval Lynch Chapel restored by the Victorians.

Brendon – Tiny village – population with Countisbury around 200 – in large parish that includes heathland of Brendon Common. Its parish church, dedicated to the Irish saint Brendan, said to have discovered America, is nearly 2 miles away.

Brendon Hill – Remains of the area's mining heyday – Burrow Farm Engine House, mine ruins, cottages, and steep mineral railway incline down to Comberow – can be explored on foot, parking at nearby Ralegh's Cross lay-by. Civilisations collide with the ancient Naked Boy standing stone close by the former engine house and trackbed of the mineral line.

Brendon Two Gates – Named for the double gate at one of the gaps that John Knight had to leave in his long boundary wall to let old roads through, and distinct from the old moorgates. Now a cattle grid and a good start point for walks eastwards down Hoccombe Water or westwards towards the Hoar Oak Tree following the county boundary.

Bridgetown – Hamlet in tranquil Exe Valley midway between Wheddon Cross and Dulverton with old mill, packhorse bridge and riverside cricket ground with thatched pavilion. A lovely walk along the river leads to Winsford.

Brompton Regis – Sleepy village, with interesting church, in the Brendon Hills. The king signified by *Regis* is thought to have been William the Conqueror who claimed the estate for himself as it had been held by King Harold's mother. But legend also claims King Stephen visited – probably the only reigning monarch to do so.

Bury – Pretty hamlet in Haddeo Valley, near Dulverton, known for its ford and narrow packhorse bridge, both best crossed on foot rather than car. Bury Castle, an iron age hill-fort later reused for a motte-and bailey castle, is nearby.

The ford and packhorse bridge at Bury – a scene little changed over centuries.

Carhampton – Large village on edge of the National Park near Dunster, said to be named after Celtic St Carantoc who rid the area of one or more fiery dragons. Also has legends of King Arthur and was held by King Alfred. On Old Twelfth Night (17 January) the ancient custom of apple wassailing is carried on. Pronounced C'rampton.

Challacombe – The name means cold valley and this moorland village is the nearest to Exmoor's most impressive menhir the Longstone on a wet, desolate spot between Wood Barrow and Chapman Barrows.

The Chains – Wild central ridge, literally the chine or backbone, reaching its highest point at Chains Barrow 1599ft (487m). The rivers Exe, Barle and West Lyn rise here amid blanket bog where walkers sometimes report the strange sensation of the ground bouncing underfoot. The most direct approach to Chains Barrow is along the Macmillan Way from the B3358; various trails and paths from the latter and B3223 converge at Exe Head, leading north to the Hoar Oak Tree or west to Pinkworthy Pond.

Chapman Barrows – Exmoor's largest collection of Bronze Age barrows – 11 in all – lying mainly on Challacombe Common. Reach them via a long track from Parracombe or along the wild Chains ridge. Also walk (access has been agreed with the landowner) via a Bronze Age ridgeway to Exmoor's largest standing stone, the Longstone – 9ft (3m) high) – and Longstone Barrow, or by means of a circular walk from Breakneck Hole via Wood Barrow.

Pack of Cards.

Combe Martin – Named after Martin de Tours, friend of William the Conqueror, this large straggling village in the Umber Valley claims to have the longest street in England. Unmissable is the Pack O'Cards pub built for George Ley in 1690, said to have been paid for with winnings from a card game. It has four storeys, 13 doors on each floor, 52 windows and 52 doors, as per the number of cards in a deck. Though outside the National Park it has an ENP Visitor Centre and the geologically interesting beach and nearby Wild Pear Beach are within the boundaries. The last engine from its silver mining days can be seen from Knap Down.

Countisbury – Hamlet at the top of famous hill of same name with church and sixteenth-century former Blue Ball Inn, now the Sandpiper. Walk to the Foreland for breathtaking view from Countisbury Common 1000 feet (305m). Be warned, the walk up from the lighthouse on Exmoor's most northerly point rises 800ft (243m) in three-quarters of a mile! Also views to the Iron Age rampart to the west on Wind Hill and east to short-lived Roman fortlet of Old Burrow Hill.

County Gate – Stands on Somerset/Devon border and west is Countisbury Hill, sharing the honours with infamous Porlock Hill for steepness. Good point from which to explore Doone Country and Glenthorne estate.

Cow Castle – Perhaps best known and most accessible of the Iron Age hill-forts on natural hillock in Barle Valley. The rocky outcrop close by is called the Calf. The walk from Simonsbath or Landacre also passes the ruins of Wheal Eliza. A diversion of the Two Moors Way takes you past Horsen and Wintershead, two of John Knight's model farms.

Culbone – Tiny hamlet in deep shaded valley, famous for smallest parish church in England and for inspiring Coleridge's 'Kubla Khan'.

Doone Country – The area around Badgworthy Water where Blackmore's *Lorna Doone* was set, and fact and fiction collide. Hoccombe Combe, with its deserted medieval settlement is the 'Doone Valley' of the book, though Lank Combe more closely fits Blackmore's descriptions and is home to the Waterslide where its hero John Ridd meets Lorna. Both are a walk of 4 or 5 miles (7k) through beautiful heathland and ancient woodland of crooked oaks, starting from Malmsmead.

Dulverton – Charming and quietly adaptable little town, once busy with cloth making, for long a centre for hunting and fishing with more than 20 hotels and inns catering for those pursuits; now also a centre for arts, crafts and antiques. Its former Union Workhouse houses the headquarters of Exmoor National Park.

Dunkery Beacon – Highest point of Exmoor's central ridge – and Exmoor itself – at 1705ft (519m), with views of up to 13 counties, as well as Horner Wood and Horner Water. Also the site of a former fire beacon and still used thus to mark special occasions. Easy walks to the summit from Dunkery Gate and Rex Stile Head. This ridge was almost certainly an ancient trackway and hereabouts are Bronze Age barrows of Rowbarrows, Kit Barrows and Robin How and Joaney How (How is the Norse name for a barrow). Spot wildflowers such as tormentil, blue heather speedwell, heath spotted orchid, bog pimpernel and milkwort.

Dulverton.

Dunster – Gem of a medieval village, almost too attractive for its own good as hordes of visitors can make it overcrowded at times. Wool brought prosperity in medieval times when the town also boasted a harbour. The famous octagonal Yarn Market dates to the early seventeenth century wool but was built when the wool industry was already waning. Other fine medieval buildings include the Priory church, tithe barn, dovecote and Luttrell Arms, once owned by the Abbots of Cleeve. The castle, home of the Luttrells for 600 years and now National Trust owned is well worth visiting, along with its restored watermill. There are also lovely walks on Gallox Hill to the east and Grabbist Hill to the west. Numerous teashops to refresh on return.

The so-called Nunnery at Dunster.

Exford.

Exford – Village truly at the heart of Exmoor, set round tranquil village green, but busy hunting, fishing and walking centre, with hotels, guesthouses and a youth hostel. The ford of its name was spanned by a bridge featured in Lorna Doone as the scene for an exploit of highwayman Tom Faggus. A path leads northwards from Exford Common to Dunkery Beacon.

Hawkridge – Lonely village, one of the highest on Exmoor, perching loftily above Dane's Brook and River Barle where it is crossed by Tarr Steps below. Took precedence over Withypool in early medieval times, having the parish church. In 1978 it was cut off for ten days by a freak blizzard.

Hoar Oak Tree – Ancient boundary mark of the former Royal Forest though present one was planted in 1916/17, the third in over 300 years. From Brendon Two Gates follow John Knight's boundary for 2 miles or start at Exe Head Bridge on B3223, follow Macmillan Way West to Exe Head then head north along Tarka Trail/Two Moors Way.

Horner – Hamlet with woods that are part of a National Nature Reserve, with red deer, rare lichens and ancient oaks. Its name is said to come from Saxon *hwrnwr*, the snorer, on account of its gurgling stream!

Luccombe – Pretty National Trust village, set among trees at foot of Robin How, with lovely church and thatched cottages.

Luxborough – Scattered village between Brendon and Croydon Hills, with church with unusual saddleback tower and remnants of iron mining. Good centre for walks.

Lynton and Lynmouth – The twin villages are famous for the spectacular coastal scenery that earned the epithet 'Little Switzerland'. Though the Park's main town and tourist honeypot, Lynton retains old-world charm with its mixture of Victorian and Swiss-style architectural designs and the cliff-railway, still busy and gleaming since 1890. Lynmouth, nestling peacefully amid gigantic cliffs and spectacular wooded gorges of the East and West Lyn, appears little changed from its days as a fishing village and port, despite the devastation of the 1952 flood – 'Lyn' is appropriately Old English (hlynn) for torrent – thanks to sensitive rebuilding. The rebuilt Rhenish Tower is a replica of a tower on the Rhine.

The amazing Lynton-Lynmouth cliff railway.

Malmsmead – Hamlet at heart of Lorna Doone country, with much-photographed ford and bridge. Walk along Badgworthy Water which forms the Devon/Somerset border into Doone country. Exmoor Natural History Society's Field Centre is just over the bridge. Blackmore's memorial stone lies along the path from here to Doone Valley.

Molland – Working estate village just off the Park boundary, much of it owned by one family from the 1400s to present day. Perpendicular church with Georgian interior, historic coaching inn and thatched and slated cob cottages.

Monksilver – Pretty village set in beautiful valley on edge of the Park. Silver derives from Latin *silva* for woodland. En route is sixteenth-century Combe Sydenham, home to Sir Francis Drake's second wife, now with restored medieval court room, country park, Drake's 'cannonball' and many legends. Once owned by the Notleys, whose name is still that of Monksilver's fine pub, the Notley Arms.

Nettlecombe – Another of Exmoor's scattered settlements, with beautiful church. Its sixteenth-century Court was once home to the Trevelyan family and is now a field studies centre.

North Molton – Straggling, once-properous village just outside National Park, 'a busy town when South Molton was vuzzy down'. All Saints church with imposing 90ft tower recalls glory days of wool wealth and episodic copper and iron mining.

Oare – Hamlet, referred to in Domesday Book as Are. Its four-teenth-century church – with later tower – is essential visiting for *Lorna Doone* addicts, as the place where Lorna was shot.

Parracombe – Village in the valley of the River Heddon. Its ancient church of St Petrock was replaced by a building nearer the centre of the village but retains a perfectly preserved Georgian interior.

Porlock – Once an important port until the sea receded, now a busy village with attractive mix of thatched cottages, Victorian and other building styles, set in a natural bowl at foot of notoriously steep Porlock Hill. The ancient parish church with its distinctive trun-cated spire is interesting, as is Doverhay House museum. Poet Robert Southey was a visitor to the Ship Inn.

Porlock Weir – Picturesque hamlet a mile and a half along the road from Porlock to the sea. Once a small, working harbour, enclosed with lock gates, it is now mainly used by pleasure craft. The shingle ridge and groynes are much loved by artists; the view across the bay is to Hurlstone Point.

Porlock Weir nestles against a precipitous drop of almost 1400ft (450 metres) and has always had an 'end of the world' feel about it.

Roadwater – Straggling village in Old Cleeve parish. See hand-made paper being crafted at Two Bridges paper mill with recently restored working water wheel. Lovely walks hereabouts.

Selworthy – Utterly chocolate-box village, with ornate thatched cottages around a village green, largely created by Thomas Acland for his Holnicote estate workers, now National Trust owned. Beautiful medieval church with views across Porlock Vale to Dunkery and lovely woodland walks.

Simonsbath – Highest village on Exmoor and very easy to miss though all roads point here. Created by Knights in nineteenth century, it is pronounced Simmonsbath and thought to mean the place where Sigmund's path crossed the Barle. Now has restored sawmill, pub and tearooms and is popular start point for walks along the Barle, also good for picnics.

Stoke Pero – Isolated and scattered village of a few farmsteads. Pero comes from the name of the family who held land here about 1300.

Tarr Steps – Ancient clapper bridge of unknown antiquity, one of the most popular spots on Exmoor and best avoided at peak times. The name may derive from tor, the exposed slabs of rock found on moorland summits, or *tochar* the Celtic word for a causeway. Lovely walks through woodlands that are Sites of Special Scientific Interest and newly designated a National Nature Reserve.

Timberscombe – Village whose Saxon name means 'wooded valley' with church dedicated to St Petrock.

Treborough – Tiny settlement standing at 998ft (304m), once with important slate quarries. The name means 'place of a waterfall' or, alternatively, woodland.

Trentishoe – Tiny village near Heddon's Mouth, whose church still has its musicians' gallery.

Twitchen – Hamlet nestling on southern edge of the Park, its name deriving from 'twicene' a meeting of the ways.

Valley of Rocks – Stunning streamless valley west of Lynton, with legends galore, stupendous views, spooky rock formations, remains of prehistoric settlement and wild goats. Take the South West Coast Path from Lynton for maximum drama.

Watersmeet – Where Hoar Oak Water and the East Lyn meet. Popular beauty spot and Site of Special Scientific Interest with footpaths, rare ferns and flowers, and tea gardens/visitor centre in former nineteenth-century lodge built by the Hallidays of Glenthorne. Amazingly it is still possible to have it to yourself away from popular times.

Wheddon Cross – Highest point on the A396 between Exmoor and the Brendon Hills, and crossroads of the Exe Valley turnpike from 1810. The Rest and Be Thankful Inn recalls days when four-horse coaches laboured to negotiate the climb to 950ft (290m) above sea level.

Winsford – Undoubtedly one of the most beautiful villages in England with much-photographed thatched Royal Oak inn and at least seven bridges and a ford over the Winn Brook and River Exe. Good start and even better end point for lovely walks with views of Winsford slumbering peacefully in the Exe Valley and bucketloads of history up on Winsford Hill. Birthplace of Labour politician Ernest Bevin.

Winsford.

Withypool – Ancient former 'capital' of the moor, 4 miles along the Barle from Tarr Steps. R.D. Blackmore is said to have written part of *Lorna Doone* whilst staying at the Royal Oak inn, where reputedly the log fire is never allowed to go out. A favourite haunt of anglers. and ideal walking centre with walks fanning out in all directions –

and always worth making sure they are circular! Withypool Hill to the west has one of Exmoor's very few stone circles and skylarks can be heard.

Wimbleball Lake – reservoir for large part of Devon and Somerset, created by damming of Haddeo with 161ft (50m) high dam. Set in woodland and meadow it has miles of beautiful walks and a rustic trail, nature reserve, ponies, sailing and fishing. Perfect for picnics.

Woody Bay – Hamlet once destined to be tourist resort and with legends of ghosts and smugglers, but now all quiet. A tricky track leads to a small beach with a lime kiln, lime burner's cottage and Hanging Water waterfall.

Further Information

Details of guided walks and those linked with bus routes, can be found in *Exmoor Visitor*, at ENP Visitor Centres and Village Information Agencies. The National Trust also publishes details of suggested walks on their land. Walking, riding and cycling circular routes appear regularly in *Exmoor – The Country Magazine*. OS map Explorer OL9 covers Exmoor National Park.

Two Moors Way – walk crossing Exmoor and Dartmoor, from Lynmouth to Ivybridge – tel. Devon Tourist Information Service for details 0870 60 85 531

SouthWest Coast Path – Exmoor section is from Minehead to Combe Martin – tel. 01752 896237 for details or visit www.swcp.org.uk

Macmillan Way – sponsored by the national charity for cancer relief – tel. 01789 740852 for details or visit www.macmillanway.org

Exmoor Scenic Walks – series of trails in Exmoor National Park with Shirley and Mike Hesman – tel. 01271 862421

Riding – point-to-points are a major fixture in the Exmoor calendar, along with gymkhanas, shows and other events organised by hunts and local societies. The British Horse Society has a guide to circular trails for riders as part of their Access and Rights of Way (ARROW) strategy, plus a *Bed and Breakfast for Horses* guide.

Cycling – offroad cycling is permitted on all bridleways but may conflict with walkers and horse-riders so keeping to designated routes is encouraged. Leaflets for designated routes are available from ENP Visitor Centres and the National Trust.

Exmoor National Park Authority – tel. 01398 323150, www.exmoor-nationalpark.gov.uk

Exmoor Society – tel/fax. 01398 323335

BIBLIOGRAPHY AND FURTHER READING

Acland, Anne *A Devon Family – The Story of the Aclands* Phillimore 1981

Binding, Hilary *Enjoying Exmoor* Exmoor Books 1999

Bonham-Carter, Victor *A Filthy Barren Ground – Exmoor in the 1850s* Exmoor Microstudy B-C Press 1998

Bourne, Hope *A Little History of Exmoor* and *Wild Harvest* Exmoor Books 2001

Burton, Roger A. *The Heritage of Exmoor* Burton 1989

Burton, S.H. *Exmoor* Robert Hale 1978

Beazley, David *Exmoor Rangers' Favourite Walks* Exmoor Books 1999

Delderfield, Eric *New Brief Guide to Exmoor* ERD Publication 1968

Eardley-Wilmot, Hazel *Ancient Exmoor* The Exmoor Press 1983 and *Yesterday's Exmoor* Exmoor Books 1990

Edwards, R.A. *Exmoor Geology* Exmoor Books 2000

Halliday, Ursula *Glenthorne – A Most Romantic Place* Exmoor Books 1995

Hurley. J. *Legends of Exmoor* Exmoor Press 1973

Hutton, Edward *Highways & Byways of Somerset* Macmillan & Co. 1930

Lauder, Rosemary Anne *Exmoor Travellers* Allan Sutton Publishing 1993

Page, J.Ll.W. *An Exploration of Exmoor and the Hill Country of West Somerset* Shelley & Co. 1893

Pearce, Brian *Exmoor, The Official National Park Guide* Pevensey Press 2001

Riley, Hazel and Wilson-North, Robert *The Field Archaeology of Exmoor* English Heritage 2002

Slader, J.M. *Days of Renown* Bracknell, West Country Publications 1965

Williamson, Henry *Tarka the Otter* Penguin Books 1937

Illustration: Sheila Wilkinson

High Brown Fritillary.

144